Practice Test #1

Practice Questions

Reading Test

Questions 1-6 pertain to the following passage:

Leaving

Even though Martin and Beth's steps were muffled by the falling snow, Beth could still hear the faint crunch of leaves underneath. The hushed woods had often made Beth feel safe and at peace, but these days they just made her feel lonely.

"I'm glad we decided to hike the trail, Martin. It's so quiet and pretty."
"Sure."

Beth couldn't understand how it happened, but over the past few months this silence had grown between them, weighing down their relationship. Of course, there was that thing with Mary, but Beth had forgiven Martin. They moved on. It was in the past.

"Do you want to see a movie tonight?" asked Beth. "There's a new one showing at the downtown theater."

"Whatever you want."

She wanted her husband back. She wanted the laughter and games. She wanted the late-night talks over coffee. She wanted to forget Mary and Martin together. She wanted to feel some sort of <u>rapport</u> again.

"Is everything alright, Martin?"
"I'm fine. Just tired."
"We didn't have to come; we could have stayed at home."
"It's fine."

Beth closed her eyes, tilted her head back, and breathed in the crisp air. "Fine" once meant "very good," or "precious." Now, it is a meaningless word, an excuse not to tell other people what's on your mind. "Fine" had hung in the air between them for months now, a softly falling word that hid them from each other. Beth wasn't even sure she knew Martin anymore, but she was confident that it was only a matter of time before everything was not "fine," only a matter of time before he told her...

"I have to leave."
"Huh? What?"
"I got a page. My patient is going into cardiac arrest."
"I wish you didn't have to leave."
"I'm sorry, but I have to go."
"I know."

1. It is reasonable to infer that Martin and Beth's relationship
   a. Martin recently lost his job.

- 3 -

b. Martin was unfaithful to Beth.

c. Martin works too much.

d. Martin does not want to go to the movies.

e. Beth talks too much.

2. What is Martin's relationship to Beth?
   a. Martin is Beth's boyfriend.
   b. Martin is Beth's fiancé.
   c. Martin is Beth's husband.
   d. Martin is Beth's brother.
   e. Martin is Beth's friend.

3. According to Beth, the word "fine" means:
   a. "good."
   b. "precious."
   c. "very good."
   d. "sharp."
   e. Nothing—it is a meaningless.

4. Based on the passage, it is reasonable to infer that Martin is a:
   a. mechanic.
   b. medical doctor.
   c. dentist.
   d. film director.
   e. television producer.

5. The best definition of the underlined word *rapport* is:
   a. a close relationship.
   b. a sense of well-being.
   c. a common goal.
   d. loneliness.
   e. boredom.

6. Based on Beth's perception of her and Martin's relationship, it is reasonable to infer:
   a. Martin is dissatisfied with his job.
   b. Beth wants to have a baby.
   c. Martin is going to leave Beth.
   d. Martin and Beth have not known each other long.
   e. Beth cannot forgive Martin.

Questions 7-11 pertain to the following passage:

How are Hypotheses Confirmed?

Most scientists agree that while the scientific method is an invaluable methodological tool, it is not a failsafe method for arriving at objective truth. It is debatable, for example, whether a hypothesis can actually be confirmed by evidence.

When a hypothesis is of the form "All x are y," it is commonly believed that a piece of evidence that is both x and y confirms the hypothesis. For example, for the hypothesis "All monkeys are hairy," a particular monkey that is hairy is thought to be a confirming piece of evidence for the hypothesis. A problem arises when one encounters evidence that disproves a hypothesis: while no scientist would argue that one piece of evidence proves a hypothesis, it is possible for one piece of evidence to disprove a hypothesis. To return to the monkey example, one hairless monkey out of one billion hairy monkeys disproves the hypothesis "All monkeys are hairy." Single pieces of evidence, then, seem to affect a given hypothesis in radically different ways. For this reason, the confirmation of hypotheses is better described as probabilistic.

Hypotheses that can only be proven or disproven based on evidence need to be based on probability because sample sets for such hypotheses are too large. In the monkey example, every single monkey in the history of monkeys would need to be examined before the hypothesis could be proven or disproven. By making confirmation a function of probability, one may make provisional or working conclusions that allow for the possibility of a given hypothesis being <u>disconfirmed</u> in the future. In the monkey case, then, encountering a hairy monkey would slightly raise the probability that "all monkeys are hairy," while encountering a hairless monkey would slightly decrease the probability that "all monkeys are hairy." This method of confirming hypotheses is both counterintuitive and controversial, but it allows for evidence to equitably affect hypotheses and it does not require infinite sample sets for confirmation or disconfirmation.

7. What is the main idea of the second paragraph?
   a. One hairy monkey proves the hypothesis "All monkeys are hairy."
   b. The same piece of evidence can both confirm and disconfirm a hypothesis.
   c. Confirming and disconfirming evidence affect hypotheses differently.
   d. The scientific method is not a failsafe method for arriving at objective truth.
   e. One billion monkeys is an adequate sample size for the monkey hypothesis.

8. A synonym for the underlined word, <u>disconfirmed</u>, would be:
   a. proven
   b. dissipated
   c. distilled
   d. disproven
   e. forgotten

9. Which of the following is true of hypotheses of the form "All x are y"?
   a. Something that is neither x nor y disproves the hypothesis.
   b. Something that is both x and y disproves the hypothesis.
   c. Something that is x but not y disproves the hypothesis.
   d. Something that is y but not x disproves the hypothesis.
   e. Something that is x, y, and z disproves the hypothesis.

10. In the third paragraph, why does the author discuss the "sample set" of monkeys?
    a. To show that there are significant differences between monkey species.
    b. To show that all monkeys are hairy.
    c. To show that just a few monkeys can prove the hypothesis "all monkeys are hairy."
    d. To show that practical concerns make confirmation or disconfirmation a function of probability.
    e. To show that different hypotheses can say the same thing.

11. Using the same reasoning as that in the passage, an automobile with eighteen wheels does what to the following hypothesis: "All automobiles have only four wheels"?
    a. It proves the hypothesis.
    b. It raises the hypothesis's probability.
    c. It disproves the hypothesis.
    d. It decreases the hypothesis's probability.
    e. It does not affect the hypothesis.

Questions 12-17 pertain to the following passage:

The Grieving Process

Since its formulation, Dr. Kubler-Ross' stages of grieving have been an invaluable tool in understanding how people cope with loss. Although individuals may experience the stages of grieving in varying degrees and in various progressions, the average person tends to go through the following stages when grieving: denial, anger, bargaining, depression, and acceptance. While most of these stages seem natural, many people do not understand the importance of the anger stage in the grieving process.

When a person experiences a significant loss in his or her life, experiencing anger as a result of this loss is both <u>cathartic</u> and therapeutic; in other words, anger at one's loss provides an emotional release and allows for the beginning of the healing process. By directing one's anger at a deity, fate, or even oneself, grieving people can come to realize that tragedies are seldom the fault of an individual or a higher power; rather, loss is a natural part of living that each person must experience. Trying to assign blame can allow the grieving individual to abandon his or her anger by showing that there is no-one to whom blame can be assigned. Having no-one to blame allows the bereaved to begin to heal because he or she can begin to come to terms with the necessity of loss. If an individual cannot move beyond anger, however, he or she may exhibit destructive tendencies.

There are a number of ways that people can fail to properly go through the anger stage of the grieving process. Some individuals may never find an object for their anger. These people may feel a vague, continual irritability or may react unreasonably to circumstances. Other grieving individuals may assign blame to an object but not realize that a given person or entity is blameless. This may result in a loss of religious faith, an unreasonable hatred of an individual, or even self-destructive tendencies in those individuals who blame themselves. These and other destructive consequences may be avoided if the bereaved successfully negotiate the grieving process.

Anger is not generally approved of in contemporary society because it is associated with violence, hatred, and destruction. Anger does, however, have its place—it is a natural and healthy step in the grieving process. Without experiencing this vital stage, it is difficult, if not impossible, to begin to move past tragedy.

12. Which of the following is true according to the passage?
    a. Grieving individuals can be self-destructive.
    b. Grieving individuals need therapy.
    c. People who suffer tragedy never fully heal.
    d. Crying is a natural consequence of loss.
    e. People should always avoid anger.

13. What is the main idea of the first paragraph?
    a. Depression is a normal and important part of the grieving process.
    b. No-one grieves in the same way.
    c. Not moving through the anger stage of the grieving process can produce destructive consequences.
    d. Anger is the least important part of the grieving process.
    e. Many people do not understand the importance of anger to the grieving process.

14. Based on the passage, the underlined word, "cathartic," most likely means:
    a. having to do with anger
    b. unhealthy
    c. healthy
    d. related to emotional release
    e. depressing

15. How does anger help individuals heal?
    a. It allows the bereaved to more quickly enter into the "bargaining" stage of the grieving process.
    b. It helps people understand that tragedy is usually blameless.
    c. It helps people to lash out at others.
    d. Anger raises immune-responses to infection.
    e. Anger helps people forget grief.

16. Why is anger not generally approved of in contemporary society?
    a. Anger does not serve any positive purpose.
    b. Anger makes people nervous.
    c. Angry people are unpleasant.
    d. Anger is associated with violence, hatred, and destruction.
    e. All of the above.

17. Which of the following are possible consequences of failing to go through the anger stage of the grieving process?
   a. Vague, continued irritability.
   b. The loss of religious faith.
   c. Self-destructive tendencies.
   d. All of the above.
   e. None of the above.

Questions 18-23 pertain to the following passage:

I Think, Therefore, I Am

When the philosopher René Descartes famously declared "I think, therefore, I am," many took his assertion to be a self-evident truth; after all, how can one dispute the fact that if he or she is thinking, then he or she exists? Careful examination of this proposition reveals that it is not as self-evident as once thought.

For any given characteristic, x, there must be something that has that characteristic. For example, there is no such thing as "red"; there are red things like red paper, red hair, red apples, and so forth. When Descartes says "I think, therefore, I am," he asserts that if thinking exists, there must be something that is doing the thinking. Since Descartes is thinking, he must exist. This seems clear enough, but looking at the argument more closely reveals some interesting and problematic features.

Even though Descartes convincingly argues that if thinking exists, there must be something that is doing the thinking, he cannot make the leap that he, Descartes, exists. The person "Descartes" has many characteristics: he is a given height, weighs a certain amount, has certain memories, and so forth. Descartes' proposition, "Cogito ergo sum," only demonstrates that something is thinking, not that Descartes is thinking. The most that can be concluded, then, is that if thinking exists, there is something that is thinking; no further conclusions may be drawn from Descartes' proposition.

While Descartes' famous proposition has limited applicability, its importance to Western philosophy must not be undervalued. Many of Descartes' successors like Hume, Berkeley, and Kant struggled with the problems associated with the cogito (what Descartes' proposition came to be known as), and many continue to explore the ways that the existence of thinking and consciousness reveal truths about the world.

18. The purpose of the second paragraph is to:
   a. provide contextual information.
   b. explain Descartes' argument.
   c. explore "redness."
   d. ridicule Descartes.
   e. highlight the continued importance of Descartes' argument.

19. In the third paragraph, the author discusses Descartes' height, weight, and memories to:
    a. show that these characteristics do not exist.
    b. demonstrate that logic does not always work in cases where consciousness is discussed.
    c. underscore the fact that Descartes' existence and his characteristics cannot be proven by his argument.
    d. devalue the importance physical characteristics.
    e. show that Descartes did not adequately explore quantity and measurement.

20. What does "*cogito ergo sum*" most likely mean?
    a. "For every thought there is a thing."
    b. "I am, therefore, you are."
    c. "To talk is to be."
    d. "To exist is to think"
    e. "I think, therefore, I am."

21. Based on the passage, it is likely that Hume, Berkeley, and Kant are:
    a. philosophers.
    b. Descartes' ancestors.
    c. artists.
    d. scientists.
    e. historians.

22. According to the passage, what can be concluded from the proposition "I think, therefore I am?"
    a. Myself, with all of my characteristics, exists.
    b. The external world exists.
    c. Color is an illusion.
    d. There is something that thinks.
    e. Nothing can be concluded from the proposition.

23. This passage is:
    a. mocking.
    b. dismissive.
    c. balanced.
    d. biased.
    e. praising.

Questions 24-29 pertain to the following passage:

How to Choose and Purchase an Automobile
Choosing and purchasing an automobile in a volatile market is not simply a function of color or engine preference; on the contrary, consumers need to treat the purchase of an automobile as the investment that it is—they need to research the pros and cons of owning various automobiles, and they need to make an informed decision before arriving at the dealership. Failure to properly prepare for such an investment can result in an unnecessary economic loss for the consumer.

While there are many pros and cons associated with automobile ownership, many consumers do not adequately research the specifics benefits and <u>detriments</u> associated with purchasing a particular vehicle. One of the most common concerns is economic: how much does it cost to own a particular vehicle over time? The cost of ownership is not limited to purchase price; it also includes things like insurance prices, repair costs, and gas-consumption. While a given vehicle may have a higher sticker price, its low cost of ownership may, over time, offset this expense. Conversely, a vehicle may have a low sticker price but a high cost of ownership over time. Accordingly, consumers should thoroughly research vehicles before they visit an automobile dealership.

There are numerous ways for consumers to research the cost (defined broadly) of a vehicle before they ever step inside that vehicle. Most simply, there are a number of publications that list the relative depreciations of automobiles over time. Consumers can use these publications to track how a particular model tends to lose value over time and choose that vehicle that best retains its value. Consumers can also go directly to a manufacturer's websites to compare gas mileage or the cost of replacement parts. Furthermore, insurance agents can provide insurance quotes for customers before a purchase is made. Awareness of factors such as these can also simplify the purchasing process.

When a consumer is finally ready to purchase a vehicle, he or she is less likely to be pressured by a salesperson if he or she is equipped with the relevant data for that purchase; i.e., if a consumer knows the long-term costs of a particular vehicle, he or she is less likely to be swayed by short-term or cosmetic benefits. Arriving at a dealership unprepared can result in an impulse purchase which, in turn, may result in increased automotive expenditure over time. Conducting even a modicum of research, however, can potentially save the average automotive consumer thousands of dollars in the long-run.

24. Why should consumers treat an automobile purchase as an investment?
    a. Automotive stock is traded on various stock exchanges.
    b. If consumers do not treat it as an investment, they may unnecessarily lose money.
    c. Vehicles may appreciate over time.
    d. Owning a vehicle has potential risks and rewards.
    e. Many vehicles may be repaired and sold for a profit.

25. Based on the passage, which of the following is another word for the underlined word "detriments?"
    a. purchases
    b. cons
    c. benefits
    d. investments
    e. pros

26. According to the passage, which of the following is true?
   a. Vehicles with a higher sticker price always cost the most over time.
   b. SUV's are always expensive to own.
   c. Red automobiles are more expensive because their insurance rates are higher.
   d. Automobiles with a lower sticker price always cost the most over time.
   e. Sticker price does not determine the overall cost of a vehicle.

27. What does the cost of ownership of a vehicle include?
   a. purchase price
   b. gas consumption
   c. cost of repairs
   d. insurance
   e. All of the above.

28. If a consumer conducts research before going to an automobile dealership, he or she is:
   a. more likely to be swayed by high-pressure sales techniques.
   b. less likely to be swayed by the short-term benefits associated with a particular vehicle.
   c. more likely to be dismissive with, or rude to, salespeople.
   d. less likely to be concerned with insurance rates associated with a particular vehicle.
   e. None of the above.

29. According to the passage, what information can consumers find on a manufacturer's website that can help them make a sound financial decision?
   a. The gas mileage of a particular vehicle.
   b. The different colors offered for a particular vehicle.
   c. The cost of replacement parts.
   d. Answer A and Answer C
   e. All of the above.

Questions 30-34 pertain to the following passage:

School Days

As Bill lumbered up the stairs to Hendrickson Hall he wondered if he was up to this—twenty years was a long time, and maybe he had forgotten the ropes. He wasn't even sure if this was the right building.

"Uh, hey, uh…is this where the Biology labs are?" stammered Bill to a young woman clad all in black. "She's probably an art student," thought Bill.

"No. This is, like, Hendrickson Hall. You know…the English building."

Bill neither appreciated the girl's eye-rolling nor the snooty way she emphasized "English." Nevertheless, he mumbled a "thank-you" and hurried towards the student center to check his schedule and the campus map.

"Martha, if you weren't gone, you'd be able to show me around this campus lickety-split. You'd probably say, 'Bill, you big dope, can't you find your way around a simple college? What would you do without me?'" Now that she was gone, Bill could answer such questions: Without Martha, he made do. He neither succeeded nor failed; he simply made do.

As he approached the student center doors, a group of cheerleaders approached from inside the center. Without hesitation, Bill opened a door

- 11 -

for them and stepped to the side. Ten young, attractive, laughing girls passed through the door without glancing at Bill. He felt like he should be angry or indignant, but instead, he was <u>dumbfounded</u>. He simply could not understand how one person would not think to thank, let alone acknowledge, another person who had done them a good turn. He stood there for about two minutes, silently holding the door, looking back and forth between the center and the direction of the parking lot. Bill gently closed the door, put his hands in his pockets, and began the long walk back to his car.

"I'm sorry Martha, but I can't do it. Things are just too different now. Don't be disappointed; I'll still find things to do. God, I miss you."

30. Based on the passage, exactly how old is Bill?
    a. twenty years old
    b. forty years old
    c. fifty years old
    d. seventy-five years old
    e. The passage does not state Bill's age.

31. Which of the following best describes Bill's state of mind in the passage?
    a. apathetic
    b. reflective
    c. angry
    d. ebullient
    e. confused

32. It is most reasonable to assume that Martha:
    a. left Bill for another man.
    b. died suddenly.
    c. is no longer in Bill's life.
    d. is waiting at home for Bill.
    e. is a figment of Bill's imagination.

33. Which of the following is another word for the underlined word "dumbfounded"?
    a. perplexed
    b. rationalized
    c. dilapidated
    d. entreated
    e. perseverated

34. Based on the passage, it is reasonable to assume that:
    a. Bill was once a car mechanic.
    b. Bill is a retired college professor.
    c. Bill will not return to college.
    d. Bill never really loved Martha.
    e. Bill is senile.

Reduction

Reducing liquids is a fundamental culinary skill that any aspiring chef or cook must include in his or her repertoire. A reduction, in short, is a process whereby a given liquid is slowly simmered until its volume diminishes. This <u>diminution</u> causes the flavors of the reduced liquid to intensify and sometimes sweeten. The ability to perform effective reductions is integral because recipes ranging from simple sauces to desserts may call for reductions. Learning how to perform a reduction is perhaps best demonstrated through the classic reduction called for in the recipe for chicken Marsala.

Prior to making the Marsala reduction in a chicken Marsala dish, one should dredge thin chicken breasts in flour and fry the breasts over medium heat until browned. Once the chicken has been browned, remove the chicken and set it aside. Two tablespoons of butter should be melted over medium heat in the same pan in which the chicken was browned. When the butter is melted, one cup of Marsala wine should be added to pan and heated until simmering (lightly boiling). The wine and butter should be allowed to boil down from approximately one cup to approximately one-half cup. When the sauce has reduced, one-half cup of chicken stock and the browned chicken breasts should be added to the mixture. The sauce should be brought back to a simmer and reduced by half (this should take approximately ten to fifteen minutes). When the sauce has reduced by half, it should be thick enough to adhere to the chicken. At this point, it is ready to serve.

The reduction that occurs in the above chicken Marsala recipe is fairly typical of reductions. Whether one is reducing the volume of chicken stock for a soup, or reducing balsamic vinegar or wine, the procedure is essentially the same: simmer the liquid until its volume reduces to the point where it changes the sauce's consistency. While reductions are fairly straightforward, there are some pitfalls in the process. One common mistake that people make is over boiling the sauce. If a sauce is boiled too vigorously it may scorch, which will impart a burnt, acrid taste to the sauce. Another common mistake is adding thickening agents to the sauce because the reduction is not occurring fast enough. Adding starches to the sauce to force it to thicken it will not bring out the same intensity of flavor that a reduction produces. It may also make the final sauce thick and lumpy. The process for making a reduction is simple, but it must be followed closely if one wants his or her sauce to be palatable.

35. The underlined word, diminution, most closely means:
   a. process.
   b. liquid.
   c. decrease.
   d. skill.
   e. volume.

36. According to the passage, why is the ability to perform reductions important for chefs or cooks?
    a. The ability to perform reductions demonstrates culinary skill.
    b. Restaurant customers like reductions.
    c. Reductions are popular in contemporary cuisine.
    d. Many recipes call for reductions.
    e. Employers will not hire chefs or cooks without this ability.

37. In the chicken Marsala recipe, when should butter be added to the pan?
    a. Before the chicken breasts are browned.
    b. After the chicken breasts are browned.
    c. After the wine has begun to simmer.
    d. While the chicken breasts are being browned.
    e. Butter is not added to the pan.

38. At what point does reduction occur in the chicken Marsala recipe?
    a. When the Marsala wine is reduced in half.
    b. When the butter is melted.
    c. When the wine/chicken stock mixture is reduced in half.
    d. At points A, B, and C.
    e. At points A and C.

39. Which of the following is a common mistake made when performing reductions?
    a. under boiling the sauce
    b. adding butter
    c. using starches to thicken the sauce
    d. All of the above.
    e. None of the above.

40. What function does the chicken Marsala recipe serve in the passage?
    a. It illustrates the importance of reductions.
    b. It is an example that demonstrates how to do a reduction.
    c. It is an example that demonstrates how not to do a reduction.
    d. It helps the reader relate his or her experience to the passage.
    e. It establishes the author's credibility.

Questions 41-46 pertain to the following passage:

Anxiety and Exacerbation

Anxiety is a condition that affects millions of Americans. While the direct causes of anxiety remain unclear, physiological and psychological factors have been implicated in causing and sustaining anxiety. Whatever the source of anxiety, there are a number of easily identifiable physical and psychological circumstances that may exacerbate anxiety.

Caffeine, nicotine, and stimulants in general are substances that tend to make the symptoms of anxiety worse. These substances exacerbate anxiety by raising the heartbeat and creating a spike in metabolic processes, and when this occurs, an anxious individual might make a mistaken or exaggerated self-assessment. For example, an anxious individual might believe that his or her heart is racing when it is only slightly elevated by the ingestion of nicotine or caffeine. This may result in catastrophic thoughts such as "My heart is beating too fast. I am having a heart attack." These thoughts may increase the individual's anxiety, which may increase the individual's heart rate, which may further increase anxiety, and so forth. Anxious individuals should, accordingly, try to avoid the unnecessary consumption of stimulants. In addition to physical exacerbations, there are a number of psychological processes that can make anxiety worse.

While there are various physiological factors that influence anxiety, probably the greatest exacerbation of anxiety is excessive worry. Individuals with anxiety disorders have a tendency to engage in excessive or catastrophic worry. Small events trigger trains of thought that are not based in reality and cause greater anxiety. For example, an individual arrives at work one morning and, upon seeing her boss, says "good morning." Her boss does not respond and continues to walk down the hallway. This individual may then think that because her boss did not acknowledge her greeting, she will be fired. After being fired, she will undoubtedly lose her home and end up living on the street. The fear of living on the street will, of course, create anxiety for this individual. Individuals who engage in thought processes like this can benefit from making their perspectives more realistic. In the above example, a realistic explanation for the boss's behavior could be that he or she did not hear the greeting. Reshaping one's perspective can be achieved through psychotherapy or meditation.

In terms of physiological and psychological exacerbations of anxiety, avoidance is only occasionally appropriate. In the case of physical exacerbations it is clear that avoidance is the best policy. In the case of psychological exacerbations, however, it is often more therapeutic to directly confront the causes of anxiety and attempt to modify one's worldview to diminish anxiety.

41. According to the passage, anxiety is always caused by:
   a. genetic factors.
   b. physical factors.
   c. psychological factors.
   d. environmental factors.
   e. None of the above.

42. "Exacerbate" most likely means:
   a. to remain the same.
   b. to make better.
   c. to lessen.
   d. to make worse.
   e. to renounce.

43. How can caffeine or other stimulants affect anxiety?
    a. Nicotine calms people down, which decreases anxiety.
    b. Stimulants can cause anxious people to confuse bodily processes.
    c. Caffeine counteracts the effects of anxiety.
    d. Stimulants can give anxious people heart attacks.
    e. Caffeine has no real affect on anxiety.

44. What is the function of the "employee-boss" example in the second paragraph?
    a. It shows that gender differences in the workplace can cause anxiety.
    b. It shows how small events can trigger catastrophic thinking in anxious people.
    c. It shows how anxious people believe that if something can go wrong it will.
    d. It is an example of how physiological factors can cause anxiety.
    e. It is an example of how anxious individuals cannot function in the workplace.

45. According to the passage, what are some ways in which an anxious person may reshape his or her perspective from a catastrophic one to a realistic one?
    a. through medication
    b. through behavior modification
    c. through meditation
    d. All of the above.
    e. None of the above.

46. According to the passage, when is avoidance is a good strategy for dealing with anxiety?
    a. always
    b. never
    c. when the exacerbations of anxiety are psychological
    d. when the exacerbations of anxiety are physiological
    e. when medications prove ineffective

Questions 47-51 pertain to the following passage:

Human and Artificial Intelligence
Many people take it for granted that humans are intelligent while computers are not. Is this a supportable position, however? What exactly is intelligence, and where does it come from? A side by side comparison of some of the functional abilities of humans and computers calls into question the proposition that there is, or always will be, a quantifiable difference between what human minds can do and what computers can do.

In the broadest sense, one might define "intelligence" as the ability to receive information from an external source, to process that information with reference to previously received information, and to generate appropriate outputs. Under this definition, both humans and computers are intelligent. For example, a human may learn the Pythagorean theorem, realize that this theorem is applicable to engineering, and then go on to use the theorem when constructing a deck or set of stairs. A similar program may be installed on a computer that allows the computer to perform the same function. But are the human and the computer doing the same thing? They are built so differently, how can they be the same?

Some people might object that human and artificial intelligence cannot be equated because the human brain is radically different from a computer's hardware. Such an argument is flawed, however. Just as different computers can run the same program, different people can have the same thought or mental process. If different people can have the same thought, and their brains are built differently, then it seems that physical construction is not a relevant concern in determining intelligence. One might object, however, that the idea of "programming" demonstrates that humans and computers do not have the same sort of intelligence.

Human beings have the ability to learn without direct prompting. While it is true that humans maximize their ability to learn through teaching, they are able to learn without a teacher. Computers, on the other hand, need to be built and programmed in order to learn anything. Perhaps intelligence is the ability to learn without being directly taught or programmed. This proposition neglects the idea that humans are programmed by the constitution of their brains. The human brain, for example, has the ability to acquire language built into its construction. In this sense, one might say that humans are programmed to receive the input necessary to learn French, for example. Accordingly, one cannot simply argue that computers are programmed and humans are not. Programming might not be a viable avenue for distinguishing intelligence between humans and computers.

As has been shown, the question of intelligence is not only difficult to answer, but it is also difficult to ask. One thing is clear: before one may judge whether computers are intelligent or not, one must first determine what intelligence actually is.

47. Which of the following best captures the main idea of the first paragraph?
    a. Computers are as intelligent as human beings.
    b. Intelligence cannot be quantifiably measured.
    c. It is unclear whether there is a difference between human and artificial intelligence.
    d. While there is a quantifiable difference between what humans and computers can do, it is negligible.
    e. Only human beings are intelligent; all other intelligence is illusory.

48. What function is the Pythagorean theorem example meant to serve?
    a. It demonstrates how human and artificial intelligence may be similar.
    b. It is an example of the definition of intelligence.
    c. It shows how human and artificial intelligence are cannot be reconciled.
    d. A and B
    e. A, B, and C

49. What is the main idea of the third paragraph?
    a. Differences in "programming" between humans and computers result in differences in intelligence.
    b. Different physical characteristics are irrelevant for determining intelligence.
    c. Only humans are intelligent because intelligence arose out of natural selection.
    d. Intelligence may be equated with certain physical constructions like having a brain.
    e. None of the above.

50. According to the passage, which of the following is true?
   a. If something is programmed, it has intelligence.
   b. Computers are programmed in exactly the same way that humans are.
   c. Appealing to programming as a means of distinguishing between intelligent and unintelligent entities might not work.
   d. All humans learn in the same way.
   e. Computers learn faster than humans.

51. What is the purpose of the passage as a whole?
   a. To question the idea that human and artificial intelligence is different.
   b. To show that humans are similar to computers in all relevant respects.
   c. To show that computers are intelligent.
   d. To question the purpose of intelligence.
   e. To show how artificial intelligence is actually natural.

Questions 52-56 pertain to the following passage:

Buddhism, Western Society, and the Self

In Western society, the individual self is generally prioritized over the collective self. This is evidenced in such things as the privatization of medicine and conceptions of ownership. In recent decades, however, there has been an increased tension in Western societies between institutions and ideologies that prioritize the individual and those groups that prioritize the collective. This is evidenced in the struggles that Western Buddhists face.

Central to Buddhist belief is the idea of "egolessness." While this term may seem to imply the absence of the individual ego or selfhood, this is not the case; rather, "egolessness" is a prioritization of the relationships between and among people over selfish concerns. "Egolessness" may also be thought of as an antonym of "ego-toxicity," that condition where an individual places his or her concerns before any other person or group's concerns. In Western societies, ego-toxicity is the reigning condition. Buddhists who live in such societies often find themselves caught between their ideology of egolessness and environmental ego-toxicity.

While a Western perspective might find it difficult to understand how a Buddhist could maintain egolessness in Western society, Buddhists are able to maintain such a perspective as a natural consequent of their beliefs. The Western perspective expects moral actions to be quid pro quo; to put it another way, a Westerner assumes that if he or she does something considered "good," then he or she should and will be rewarded. Buddhists, on the other hand, believe that good should be done out of compassion for all beings, and to do good is to do good for all beings, including the self. Approaching society and social action in an egoless manner has begun to become more prevalent in secular institutions and movements, such as the transition to a more socialized form of medical treatment in some Western countries. The struggle between the ego and the collective continues, however.

Buddhist practitioners show through their actions that it is possible to do good in the world without giving up one's personhood. When ego-

- 18 -

toxicity is abandoned, it is possible to care for one's self and the rest of the world through compassionate, egoless behavior.

52. What is the purpose of the first paragraph?
    a. To criticize Buddhist notions of the self.
    b. To criticize contemporary Western notions of the self.
    c. To introduce the tension between individuality and collectivity in Western society.
    d. To introduce the idea of "egolessness."
    e. To introduce the idea of "ego-toxicity."

53. According to the passage, what is "egolessness?"
    a. The complete denial of the self.
    b. The rejection of psychoanalytic notions of ego, superego, and id.
    c. The prioritization of self over others.
    d. The prioritization of relationships between and among people.
    e. Complete selfishness.

54. Which of the following best describes the purpose of the second paragraph?
    a. It introduces the distinction between "egolessness" and "ego-toxicity."
    b. It makes light of the conflicts that Buddhists in Western societies experience.
    c. It praises egolessness as the only moral way of living.
    d. It harshly denounces ego-toxicity.
    e. It shows how ego-toxicity and egolessness are two sides of the same coin.

55. Based on the passage, "quid pro quo" most likely means:
    a. "something for nothing."
    b. "good merits money."
    c. "to each his own."
    d. "something for something."
    e. "that which is best."

56. According to the passage, why do Buddhists do good deeds?
    a. Doing good brings direct, personal benefits to the person doing the action.
    b. They do good so that they may go to heaven when they die.
    c. If they do not do good, they will be reincarnated again.
    d. They do good because it makes them feel good.
    e. Doing good for one person is doing good for all beings.

Questions 57-60 pertain to the following passage:

Getting the Best Bean for Your Buck

Why should someone pay upwards of four dollars for a specialty cup of coffee when he or she could make a cup of coffee at home for mere pennies? The answer to this question is simple: people are willing to pay a higher price for specialty coffee because of superior ingredients and professional preparation. Are consumers really getting a professionally crafted superior product when they purchase a cup of coffee at a coffee house? There are a few simple questions that coffee house patrons should ask to make sure that they are getting the best bean for their buck.

"How are your coffees grown?" If a consumer is going to be expected to pay a premium price for coffee, he or she should know whether or not a particular coffee house supports industry standard growing practices. These standards include buying only shade grown, organic, free trade coffees. Shade grown coffees produce smaller batches of better quality beans. Organic certification insures a chemical free produce. Free trade means that growers are paid a fair price for their products. While these practices are now common industry standards, it is still important to make sure that your coffee house abides by them.

"How do you prepare your coffee?" Preparing an artisanal cup of coffee is time and work intensive. A higher level of automation (the more steps that are done automatically) lowers the individual product's quality. While brewing of drip coffee is largely automatic, the consumer might enquire when and where the beans are ground insofar as the best cup of coffee is made with freshly ground beans. Furthermore, the savvy consumer should take note of how espresso shots are poured. Do the café employees simply push a button on the espresso machine, or do they measure out and prepare the grinds? All of the these things provide clues as to how much a particular coffee house pays attention to, and cares about, individual cups of coffee.

While there are many other standards of quality that the consumer should be aware of, a coffee house's growing practices and the ways in which it prepares coffee can provide the consumer with a good basis by which to decide whether the price of a cup of specialty coffee is actually justified.

57. According to the passage, which of the following are industry standard growing practices?
    a. Using only manual labor to harvest coffee beans.
    b. Growing coffee on large plantations.
    c. Using shade grown coffee beans.
    d. Growing coffee in high rainfall areas.
    e. None of the above.

58. Based on the passage, which of the following provides clues about how much a coffee house cares about individual cups of coffee?
    a. When the drip coffee beans are ground.
    b. How clean the coffee bar is.
    c. The automation of the espresso machine.
    d. B and C
    e. A and C

59. According to the passage, "artisanal" most likely means:
    a. made according to exacting standards.
    b. second-rate.
    c. in demand.
    d. expensive.
    e. artistic.

60. What is the purpose of the passage as a whole?
    a. To convince consumers to make coffee at home.
    b. To attack the coffee industry giants.
    c. To show coffee consumers how to be better informed.
    d. To call for change in the coffee industry.
    e. None of the above.

Writing Skills Test

In the following passages, look for the errors in punctuation, grammar, usage and style. Then choose the correct sentence for each segment in the questions below.

Passage 1

1/A significant numbers of the worlds populations lives within 50 miles of the ocean. **2/This once inspiring juxtapositions is becoming** increasingly problematic because **3/the likelihood of raising sea levels within this century 4/are liable to threaten the once stable relationship** between man and the ocean. **5/Our impact on the planet's environment is having alarming affects on the planet** and the oceans are one place where **6/this impact is becoming more and more obvious as each year passes.**

The signs of this impact are not hard to find: **7/large fishes like sharks and tuna are disappearing and mammals like whales and polar bears are seeing their populations shrink smaller fish** and **8/crustacea are also declining in number** and **9/coral are dying; and as sea** temperatures rise and as ocean pollution spreads more broadly and deeply around the planet. **10/One powerful example of this is that approximate 90% of all the coral reefs** around the world are either **11/dead or dying, as a consequence of global warming and the pollution caused by untreated industrial wastes** flowing into our oceans. **12/The delicate relationship between coral, algae and the small fish that larger fish feed upon** is thus easily disrupted and **13/the once stable and complex entomological systems** that border our continents are now threatened.

14/Scientists disagree about weather 15/it is already to late to change the symbiotic **16/relationship between mankind and our oceans'. 17/The amount of carbon, in the atmosphere is rising,** and the means, politically and scientifically, to stabilize or diminish it are not readily at hand. **18/Consequently our planet is likely to get warm, 19/its icecap's and glacier's will melt and as it's seas rise** it may be necessary for all of us to get into lifeboats and start rowing.

Segment 1
   a. A significant numbers of the worlds population lives
   b. Significant numbers of the worlds populations live
   c. The worlds populations, in significant numbers, lives
   d. A significant number of the world's population live
   e. A significant number of the world's population lives

Segment 2
    a. This once inspiring juxtapositions is becoming
    b. This once inspiring juxtaposition are becoming
    c. These once inspiring juxtaposition's is becoming
    d. This, once inspiring juxtaposition, is becoming
    e. This once inspiring juxtaposition is becoming

Segment 3
    a. the likelihood of raising sea levels within this century
    b. the likelihood of rising sea levels within this century
    c. within this century the likelihood of raising sea levels'
    d. the likelihood of rising sea level's within this century
    e.   sea levels, rising within this century, is likely and

Segment 4
    a. are liable to threaten the once stable relationship
    b. are liable to threaten the once stable relationships
    c. is liable, to threaten the once stable relationship
    d. are liable to threaten, the once stable relationship
    e. is liable to threaten the once stable relationship

Segment 5
    a. Our impact on the planet's environment is having alarming affects on the planet
    b. Our impact on the planets environment are having alarming effects on the planet
    c. Our impact on the planet's environment is having alarming effects on the planet
    d. Our impact on the planet's environment is having alarming affects on the planet's
    e. Our impact on the planets environment is having alarming affects on the planet's

Segment 6
    a. this impact is becoming more and more obvious as each year passes.
    b. these impacts is becoming more and more obvious as each year passes.
    c. this impact is becoming more obvious each year.
    d. this impact is obvious.
    e. this impact is becoming more and more obvious as each year goes by.

Segment 7
    a. large fishes like sharks and tuna are disappearing and mammals like whales and polar bears are seeing their populations shrink smaller fish
    b. large fishes like sharks and tuna are disappearing; mammals like whales and polar bears are seeing their populations shrink; smaller fish
    c. large fishes like sharks and tuna are disappearing and mammals like whales and polar bears are shrinking. Smaller fish
    d. large fishes like sharks, and tuna, are disappearing, and mammals like whales, and polar bears, are seeing their populations shrink smaller fish
    e. large fish are disappearing and mammals are seeing their populations shrink smaller fish

Segment 8
    a. crustaceas are also declining in number
    b. crustacea is also declining in number
    c. also crustacea are declining in numbers
    d. crustacea are declining in numbers
    e. crustaceans are also declining in number

Segment 9
    a. coral are dying; and as sea temperatures rise as ocean pollution spreads more broadly and deeply around the planet.
    b. coral are dying; as sea temperatures rise and as ocean pollution spreads more broadly and deeply around the planet.
    c. coral are dying as sea temperatures rise as ocean pollution spreads more broadly and deeply around the planet.
    d. coral are dying; as sea temperatures rise as ocean pollution spreads, more broadly, and deeply, around the planet.
    e. coral are dying; as sea's temperatures rise, as ocean pollution spreads, more broadly and deeply around the planet.

Segment 10
    a. One powerful example of this is that approximate 90% of all the coral reefs
    b. One powerful example of this is because approximate 90% of all the coral reefs
    c. One powerful example of this is that approximately 90% of all the coral reef
    d. One powerful example of this is that approximately 90% of all the coral reefs
    e. One powerful example: that approximately 90% of all the coral reefs

Segment 11
    a. dead or dying, as a consequence of global warming and the pollution caused by untreated industrial wastes
    b. dead or dying as a consequence of global warming and the pollution caused by untreated industrial wastes
    c. dead or dying, as a consequence of global warming, and the pollution caused by untreated industrial wastes
    d. dead or dying consequently of global warming and the pollution caused by untreated industrial wastes
    e. dead or dying, as a consequence, of global warming and the pollution caused by untreated industrial wastes

Segment 12
    a. The delicate relationship between coral, algae and the small fish that larger fish feed upon
    b. The delicate relationship between coral, algae, and the small fish that larger fish feed upon
    c. The delicate relationship, among coral, algae and the small fish that larger fish feed upon,
    d. The delicate relationship, between coral, algae, and the small fish that larger fish feed upon
    e. The delicate relationship among coral, algae and the small fish that larger fish feed upon

Segment 13
    a. the once stable and complex entomological systems
    b. the once stable and complex ecological systems
    c. the once stable and complex endocrinal systems
    d. the once stable and complex endoplasmic systems
    e. the once stable and complex endobiotic systems

Segment 14
    a. Scientists disagree about weather
    b. Scientists, disagree about weather
    c. Scientists disagree about whether
    d. Scientists, disagree about whether
    e. Scientists disagree, about whether

Segment 15
    a. it is already to late to change
    b. it is already too late too change
    c. it is already two late too change
    d. it is already to late too change
    e. it is already too late to change

Segment 16
    a. relationship between mankind and our oceans'
    b. relationship between mankind and our oceans's
    c. relationship between mankind and our oceans
    d. relationships between mankind and our oceans
    e. relationship's between mankind and our oceans

Segment 17
    a. The amount of carbon, in the atmosphere is rising,
    b. The amounts of carbon, in the atmosphere are rising,
    c. The amount of carbon in the atmosphere is raising,
    d. The amount of carbon in the atmosphere is rising
    e. The amount of carbon, in the atmosphere is raising,

Segment 18
    a. Consequently our planet is likely to get warm,
    b. Consequently our planet is likely to get warmer
    c. Consequently our planet is likely to get warmer,
    d. Consequently our planet is likely to get warm
    e. Consequently, our planet is likely to get warmest,

Segment 19
    a. its icecap's and glacier's will melt and as it's seas rise
    b. its icecaps and glaciers will melt and as its seas rise
    c. it's icecap's and glacier's will melt and as its' seas rise
    d. its icecap's and glacier's will melt and as its seas rise
    e. it's icecap's and glacier's will melt and as it's seas rise

Segment 20: If the following sentence needs to be inserted, where should it logically go?

Unless concerted, effective political action is taken soon, it may be too late to rescue this situation.

a. at the end of the first paragraph
b. at the beginning of the last paragraph
c. between sentence 4 and sentence 5
d. at the end of the last paragraph
e. at the beginning of the first paragraph

Passage 2

Adhesives are sticky and designed **1/ to hold thing's together, 2/ so it is paradoxical** to talk about **3/ glues that are not to sticky**, that are un-glues, **4/ but that, so to speak, 5/ affectively is what tape is.** A subtle **6/ combination, of special papers and adhesives, 7/ are the foundation of masking tapes,** the transparent tapes we use to wrap presents and the removable notes that we place on doors, windows and into books that leave no residue once removed. **8/ These taken for granted unremarkable segments are, however, the result of innovative and sometimes serendipitous processes.**

A roll of **9/ tape is a curious artifice**. The tape sticks to itself **10/ so that it can be sold in rolls; rather than strips** hundreds of feet long. It also unsticks from itself when you **11/pull it off the roll and when you use it to seal a package** or bind a torn sheet of paper you can't pull it off without ruining the joint and tearing some of the paper **12/ you were trying to seal it is a subtle balance** that creates a tension that holds and lets go so easily.

It was the internal culture at an adhesives company that encouraged "intrapreneurship" that **13/ made these innovation's possible**. Intrapeneurship means that employees are allowed to devote some of their time **14/ to behaving as entrepreneurs** within the company. They are encouraged **15/ to follow through with they're own ideas. 16/ Overhearing a painter in an automobile factory complaining about the difficulty of painting cars two different colors one of these intrapeneurs developed masking tape.** How could you create a clean seam **17/ where the colors met but wear the paint also did not** bleed from one color area to another? The same engineer, Richard Drew, solved another daunting problem—that of making **18/ an adhesive stick to cellophane. That was transparent waterproof** and could be written upon. **19/ Though this cellophane tape was used for years:** it also yellowed, curled at the edges, dried out and was hard to get off the roll with a neat clean edge. All of these deficiencies lead to the invention of the serrated edge cutter and finally to the transparent, flexible, you-can-write-on them transparent tapes we use today. **20/None of them are called Drew Tape, but perhaps it should be**.

Segment 1
    a. to hold thing's together,
    b. to hold together things
    c. to hold thing's together
    d. to hold things together
    e. to hold things' together

Segment 2
    a. so it is paradoxical
    b. so it is logical
    c. so it is important
    d. so it is orthodoxical
    e. so it is logistical

Segment 3
    a. glues that are not to sticky
    b. glues that are, not too, sticky
    c. glues that are not too sticky
    d. glues that are not two sticky
    e. glues, that are not too sticky,

Segment 4
    a. but that, so to speak,
    b. but, that, so to speak
    c. but that so to speak,
    d. but that,
    e. so to speak,

Segment 5
    a. affectively is what tape is.
    b. in effect is what tape is.
    c. in affect, is what tape is.
    d. in effect, is what tape is.
    e. is what tape is.

Segment 6
    a. combination, of special papers and adhesives,
    b. combination, of special papers and adhesives
    c. combination of special papers and adhesives,
    d. combination, of special papers, and adhesives,
    e. combination of special papers and adhesives

Segment 7
    a. are the foundation of masking tapes,
    b. is the foundation of masking tapes
    c. are the foundation of masking tapes
    d. is the foundation of masking tapes,
    e. is, the foundation of masking tapes,

Segment 8
    a. This sentence is most effective left where it is.
    b. This sentence is most effective as the concluding sentence to this essay.
    c. This sentence is most effective at the end of the second paragraph.
    d. This sentence is most effective as the first sentence of the essay.
    e. This sentence is most effective at the beginning of the second paragraph.

Segment 9
    a. tape is a curious artifice.
    b. tape is a curious artifact.
    c. tape is a curious art.
    d. tape is a curious artificiality.
    e. tape is a curious art form.

Segment 10
    a. so that it can be sold in rolls; rather than strips
    b. so that it can be sold, in rolls rather than strips
    c. so that it can be sold in rolls rather than strips
    d. so, that it can be sold in rolls rather than strips,
    e. so that it can be sold in rolls, rather than strips

Segment 11
    a. pull it off the roll and when you use it to seal a package
    b. pull it off the roll when you use it to seal a package
    c. pull it off the roll but when you use it to seal a package
    d. pull it off the roll, but when you use it to seal a package
    e. pull it off the roll; when you use it to seal a package

Segment 12
    a. you were trying to seal it is a subtle balance
    b. you were trying to seal it is a subtle balance,
    c. you were trying to seal; it is a subtle balance
    d. you were trying to seal is a subtle balance
    e. ,you were trying to seal it is a subtle balance,

Segment 13
    a. made these innovation's possible.
    b. made their innovation's possible.
    c. made the innovation's possible.
    d. made these innovations possible.
    e. made this innovations possible.

Segment 14
    a. to behaving as entrepreneurs
    b. to behaving like entrepreneurs
    c. to behaving as entrepreneurs'
    d. to being as entrepreneurs
    e. to behaving as entrepreneurs,

Segment 15
    a. to follow through with they're own ideas.
    b. to follow through with there own ideas.
    c. to follow through with their own ideas.
    d. to follow through with those ideas'.
    e. to follow through with their own idea's.

Segment 16
    a. Overhearing a painter in an automobile factory complaining about the difficulty of painting cars two different colors one of these intrapeneurs developed masking tape.
    b. Masking tape was developed by one of these intrapeneurs after he overheard a painter in an automobile factory complaining about the difficulty of painting cars two different colors.
    c. One of these intrapeneurs developed masking tape overhearing a painter in an automobile factory complaining about the difficulty of painting cars two different colors.
    d. Overhearing a painter in an automobile factory complaining about the difficulty of painting cars two different colors, one of these intrapeneurs developed masking tape.
    e. One of these intrapeneurs developed masking tape; after overhearing a painter in an automobile factory complaining about the difficulty of painting cars two different colors,

Segment 17
    a. where the colors met but wear the paint also did not bleed
    b. were the colors met but wear the paint also did not bleed
    c. where the colors met but where the paint also did not bleed
    d. wear the colors met but wear the paint also did not bleed
    e. where the colors met but we're the paint also did not bleed

Segment 18
    a. an adhesive stick to cellophane. That was transparent, waterproof
    b. an adhesive stick to cellophane, that was transparent waterproof
    c. an adhesive stick to cellophane; That was transparent, waterproof
    d. an adhesive stick to cellophane. That was transparent waterproof
    e. an adhesive stick to cellophane that was transparent, waterproof

Segment 19
    a. Though this cellophane tape was used for years:
    b. Though this cellophane tape was used for years,
    c. Though this cellophane tape, was used for years
    d. Though this cellophane tape, was used for years,
    e. Though this cellophane tape, was used, for years and years,

Segment 20
    a. None of them are called Drew Tape, but perhaps it should be.
    b. None of them is called drew tape, but perhaps they should be.
    c. None of them is called Drew Tape, but perhaps it should be.
    d. None of them are called Drew Tape, but perhaps they should be.
    e. None of them is called drew tape, but perhaps it should be.

Passage 3

1/Searching for gold, the Spaniards came, to the New World. Believing in the Indian **2/legend of El Dorado; the story of a king whose body** was completely **3/covered in gold, they conquered, pillaged and burned** a continent in their pursuit of bullion. They did find **4/some gold in the lands of the Inca but their more significant find** was silver. In 1545, Indians in the Peruvian highlands discovered the Cerro Rico [rich hill], an entire **5/mountain of solid silver or containing five enormous seems of the precious metal. 6/And the** Spaniards were soon there asserting their claim to the treasures.

7/The Spaniard's greed was boundless and to extract the precious metal **8/they had conscripted the labor of Indian men** to work the mines. Labor conditions were unimaginably cruel. **9/ To enter mineshafts hundreds of feet deep, the Indians were forced,** that were dug with little regard for their safety or well-being. The shafts collapsed, there was no ventilation and **10/the air was filled with dangerous gases, the silver was processed and refined** in vats filled with poisonous mercury. **11/Exploited and despised the Indians were considered to be heathens and were treated** as a less than human species. By one estimate, every peso minted cost the lives of ten Indians. Eventually, **12/the inveterate population was so decimated 13/that African slaves were imported to take its place.**

14/By 1783 nearly 45,000 tons of silver had been extracted refined and sent to Seville. 15/The city of Potosi near the mines grew to become one of the largest cities in the Spanish Empire with nearly 200,000 inhabitants **16/in the 18th century it rivaled many of the great European cities** of the time in both wealth and population. **17/As a consequence of this enormous wealth, it flourished and became the largest** and strongest in Europe. **18/Always a threat playing a role in determining the fate of the Empire was piracy.** Ironically, Spain's power was short lived. **19/Extracting so much silver and used it so liberally that its value** began to decline with respect to other goods and the Empire was, by the beginning of the 19th century, **20/well on its way to entering the dustbin of history.**

Segment 1
- a. Searching for gold, the Spaniards came, to the New World.
- b. Searching for gold, the Spaniards came to the New World.
- c. The Spaniards came, searching for gold, to the New World.
- d. The Spaniards came to the New World searching for gold.
- e. The Spaniards came searching for gold, to the New World.

Segment 2
- a. legend of El Dorado; the story of a king whose body
- b. legend of El Dorado; the story of a king whose body
- c. legend of El Dorado. The story of a king whose body
- d. legend of El Dorado—the story of a king, whose body
- e. legend of El Dorado, the story of a king whose body

Segment 3
    a. covered in gold, they conquered, pillaged and burned
    b. covered in gold they conquered, pillaged and burned
    c. covered in gold. They conquered, pillaged and burned
    d. covered in gold. They conquered, pillaged, and burned
    e. covered in gold, they conquered, pillaged and burned,

Segment 4
    a. some gold in the lands of the Inca but their more significant find
    b. some gold in the lands' of the Inca but their more significant find
    c. some gold in the lands of the Inca, but their more significant find
    d. some gold in the land's of the Inca but their more significant find
    e. some gold in the lands' of the Inca, but there more significant find

Segment 5
    a. mountain of solid silver or containing five enormous seems of the precious metal.
    b. mountain, of solid silver ore, containing five enormous seams of the precious metal.
    c. mountain of solid silver or containing five enormous seams of the precious metal.
    d. mountain of solid silver ore containing five enormous seams of the precious metal.
    e. mountain, of solid silver ore, containing five enormous seems of the precious metal.

Segment 6
    a. And the Spaniards were soon there asserting their claim to the treasures.
    b. Soon there were the Spaniards, asserting their claim to the treasure.
    c. Soon, their were the Spaniards asserting their claim to the treasures.
    d. The Spaniards were soon they're asserting there claim to the treasure
    e. The Spaniards were soon there asserting their claim to the treasure.

Segment 7
    a. The Spaniard's greed was boundless
    b. The Spaniards' greed was boundless
    c. The Spaniards greed was boundless
    d. The Spaniards greed was boundless'
    e. The Spaniards' greed, was boundless

Segment 8
    a. they had conscripted the labor of Indian men
    b. they have conscripted the labor of Indian men
    c. they have had conscripted the labor of Indian men
    d. they conscripted the labor of Indian men
    e. they had to conscripted the labor of Indian men

Segment 9
    a. To enter mineshafts hundreds of feet deep, the Indians were forced,
    b. The Indians were forced, to enter mineshafts hundreds of feet deep,
    c. To enter mineshafts hundreds of feet deep the Indians were forced,
    d. The Indians were forced to enter mineshafts hundreds of feet deep
    e. To enter mineshafts hundreds of feet deep the Indians were forced

Segment 10
    a. the air was filled with dangerous gases, the silver was processed and refined
    b. the air was filled with dangerous gases: the silver was processed and refined
    c. the air was filled with dangerous gases; the silver was processed and refined
    d. the air was filled with dangerous gases, the silver was processed, and refined,
    e. the air was filled, with dangerous gases, the silver was processed, and refined

Segment 11
    a. Exploited and despised the Indians were considered to be heathens and were treated
    b. Exploited and despised, the Indians were considered to be heathens and were treated
    c. Exploited and despised, the Indians were considered to be heathens and were treated,
    d. Exploited, and despised, the Indians were considered to be heathens and were
    treated
    e. Exploited and despised the Indians were, considered to be heathens and were treated,

Segment 12
    a. the inveterate population was so decimated
    b. the inevitable population were so decimated
    c. the invariable population was so decimated
    d. the itinerant populations was so decimated
    e. the indigenous population was so decimated

Segment 13
    a. that African slaves were imported to take its place.
    b. that African slaves were imported to take their places.
    c. that African slaves we're imported to take their place.
    d. that African slaves, were imported to take there places.
    e. that African slaves were imported.

Segment 14: This sentence should:
    a. Remain where it is.
    b. Be placed before sentence 9.
    c. Be placed between sentence 10 and sentence 11.
    d. Be placed after sentence 15.
    e. Be placed after sentence 11.

Segment 15
    a. The city of Potosi near the mines grew to become one of the largest
    b. The city of Potosi, near the mines, grew to become one of the largest
    c. The city of Potosi, near the mines grew to become one of the largest
    d. The city of Potosi near the mines, grew to become one of the largest
    e. The city of Potosi near the mines grew, to become one of the largest

Segment 16
    a. in the 18th century it rivaled many of the great European cities
    b. in the 18th century, it rivaled many of the great European cities
    c. , in the 18th century, it rivaled many of the great European cities
    d. in the 18th century. It rivaled many of the great European cities,
    e. ; in the 18th century it rivaled many of the great European cities

Segment 17
    a. As a consequence of this enormous wealth, it flourished and became the largest
    b. As a consequence of this enormous wealth, Potosi flourished and became the largest
    c. As a consequence of this enormous wealth Potosi flourished and became the largest
    d. As a consequence of this enormous wealth, the Spanish Empire flourished and
    became the largest
    e. As a consequence of this enormous wealth the Spanish Empire flourished and became
    the largest

Segment 18
    a. Always a threat playing a role in determining the fate of the Empire was piracy.
    b. Always a threat, playing a role in determining the fate of the Empire was piracy.
    c. Always a threat piracy played a role in determining the fate of the Empire.
    d. Always a threat, piracy played a role in determining the fate of the Empire.
    e. Piracy was always a threat playing a role in determining the fate of the Empire.

Segment 19
    a. Extracting so much silver and used it so liberally that its value
    b. Extracting so much silver and using it so liberally that its value
    c. It extracted so much silver and used it so liberally that its value
    d. To extract so much silver and using it so liberally that its value
    e. Liberally extracting and using so much silver that its value

Segment 20
    a. well on its way to entering the dustbin of history
    b. well on its' way to entering the dustbin of history
    c. well on their ways to entering the dustbin of history
    d. well on it's way to entering the dustbin of history
    e. well on their way to entering the dustbin of history

Math Test

1. A warehouse club member purchased flooring for $27.18 per box. The warehouse club reported that the member had saved over $250 by purchasing the flooring from them rather than from the local retailer who was selling it for $61.04 per box. What is the minimum number of boxes of flooring the member would have to purchase to save over $250?
   a. 7
   b. 8
   c. 27
   d. 33
   e. 34

2. 31–27+12–23–(–25)+(–6)=
   a. -62
   b. -38
   c. -26
   d. 8
   e. 12

3. Find 32% of 750.
   a. 24000
   b. 2343.75
   c. 240
   d. 23.4375
   e. 0.04267

4. Solve for x: $4 - 3x > 7$.
   a. $x < -1$
   b. $x < 1$
   c. $x = 0$
   d. $x > -1$
   e. $x > 1$

5. $\sqrt[3]{125} - \sqrt{16}$
   a. $\sqrt[6]{109}$
   b. $\sqrt[3]{109}$
   c. $\sqrt{109}$
   d. 1
   e. 3

6. $2^{\log_3 9} =$
    a. 3
    b. 4
    c. 5
    d. 6
    e. 12

7. $\dfrac{5!3!}{6!} =$
    a. 1
    b. $1\frac{1}{3}$
    c. $2\frac{1}{2}$
    d. 3
    e. 21

8. Find the value of x.

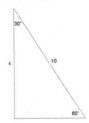

    a. $\dfrac{10\sqrt{3}}{3}$
    b. $\dfrac{10\sqrt{2}}{2}$
    c. $5\sqrt{3}$
    d. $5\sqrt{2}$
    e. 5

9. $48 \div 1.2 =$
    a. 3.4
    b. 4
    c. 34
    d. 40
    e. 57.6

10. Solve for x: $\frac{2}{5} + \frac{3}{4} + x = 2$

    a. $-\frac{3}{20}$

    b. $-\frac{3}{10}$

    c. $\frac{13}{9}$

    d. $\frac{7}{10}$

    e. $\frac{17}{20}$

11. $\dfrac{2x^2 + x - 6}{x + 2} =$

    a. (2x-6)
    b. (2x-3)
    c. (2x-2)
    d. (2x+2)
    e. (2x+3)

12. Which is the graph of $3x - y = -2$?

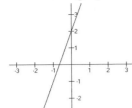

a.

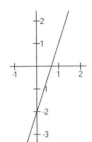

b.

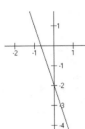

c.

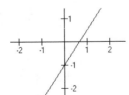

d.

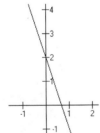

e.

13. Use the quadratic formula to solve the equation $3x^2 - 6x + 2 = 0$.

a. $\dfrac{3 \pm i\sqrt{3}}{3}$

b. $\dfrac{-3 \pm i\sqrt{3}}{3}$

c. $\dfrac{3 \pm \sqrt{3}}{3}$

d. $\dfrac{-3 \pm \sqrt{3}}{3}$

e. $\dfrac{3 \pm \sqrt{3}i}{3}$

14. Simplify: $\dfrac{\sin^2 \theta}{\cos^2 \theta} + \sin^2 \theta + \cos^2 \theta =$

a. $\sin \theta$

b. $\cos \theta$

c. $\tan \theta$

d. $\sec \theta$

e. $\csc \theta$

15. $\dfrac{\left(3^2\right)^4}{27} =$

a. 27

b. 48

c. 144

d. 243

e. 729

16. A home improvement store rents its delivery truck for $19 for the first 75 minutes and $4.75 for each additional $\frac{1}{4}$ hour. If a customer rented the truck at 11:10 a.m. and returned the truck at 1:40 p.m. the same day, what would his rental cost be?

a. $47.50

b. $42.75

c. $38.00

d. $23.75

e. $19.00

17. Factor the equation $12x^4 - 27x^3 + 6x^2$.

a. $3x^2(4x-1)(x-2)$

b. $3x^2(4x+1)(x+2)$

c. $3x^2(4x+1)(x-2)$

d. $3x^2(4x-2)(x-1)$

e. $3x^2(4x+2)(x+1)$

18. Solve the system of equations: $\begin{cases} 3x - y = 10 \\ 2x + 3y = 3 \end{cases}$

a. (-1, -3)
b. (-1, 3)
c. (3, 1)
d. (3, -1)
e. (-3, -1)

19. Given a line with slope $m = -2$ that passes through the point (-3, 4), find the equation of the line in standard form.

a. $2x + y - 2 = 0$

b. $2x - y - 2 = 0$

c. $2x + y + 2 = 0$

d. $y = 2x + 2$

e. $y = -2x - 2$

20. $6 + 4 \div 2 - 3 =$
   a. -10
   b. 2
   c. 3.5
   d. 5
   e. 7

21. The formula for calculating simple interest is given as $A = P(1 + nr)$, where A is the final account balance, P is the initial principal, n is the number of years the money is invested, and r is the rate of interest. Find A when $P = \$1000$, $n = 3$, and $r = 5\%$.
   a. $1150
   b. $1500
   c. $2000
   d. $4050
   e. $16,000

22. Find the distance between points P (-3, 4) and Q (1, 6).

    a. $2\sqrt{2}$

    b. $2\sqrt{3}$

    c. $2\sqrt{5}$

    d. $3\sqrt{2}$

    e. $5\sqrt{2}$

23. Which is the graph of $2x^2 + 2y^2 = 50$?

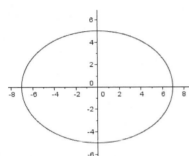

a.

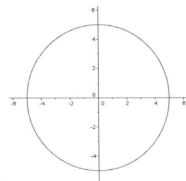

b.

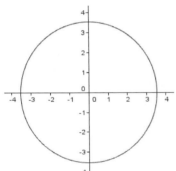

c.

d.

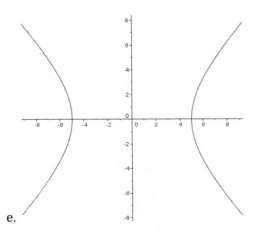

e.

24. Given the function $f(x) = 2x^2 - x + 2$, find the value of $f(y-1)$.

   a. $2y^2 - y - 3$

   b. $2y^2 - 2y + 3$

   c. $2y^2 - 2y - 5$

   d. $2y^2 - 5y + 3$

   e. $2y^2 - 5y + 5$

25. Given $\cot \theta = \frac{3}{4}$ and $\cos \theta \langle 0$, find the value of $\sin \theta$.

   a. $\frac{3}{5}$

   b. $\frac{4}{5}$

   c. $\frac{4}{3}$

   d. 3

   e. 4

26. Find the value of x if $\dfrac{3}{x} = \dfrac{9}{13}$.

   a. $\frac{1}{3}$

   b. $\frac{3}{13}$

   c. $\frac{13}{3}$

   d. $\frac{13}{9}$

   e. $\frac{27}{13}$

27. John ran a mile in 6 minutes 15 seconds. If Joe ran at an average speed of 168 inches per second, Jim ran at an average speed of 875 feet per minute, and Jeremy ran at an average speed of 10 miles per hour. Who ran faster than John?

   a. Joe only

   b. Jim only

   c. Jeremy only

   d. Jim and Jeremy

   e. Joe, Jim, and Jeremy

28. Given $m = 5$ and $n = -4$, find the value of $2m^2 + 3mn - 2n^2$.

   a. -74

   b. -42

   c. -24

   d. 78

   e. 104

29. $\sqrt{12n^5} - 3n\sqrt{3n^3} =$

   a. $-n^2\sqrt{3n}$

   b. $n^2\sqrt{3n}$

   c. $3n^2\sqrt{3n}$

   d. $4n^2\sqrt{3n}$

   e. $7n^2\sqrt{3n}$

30. Find all possible solutions of the equation $2x^2 + 3x = 4$.

   a. $\frac{-3 \pm i\sqrt{23}}{4}$

   b. $\frac{-3 \pm i\sqrt{41}}{4}$

   c. $\frac{-3 \pm \sqrt{23}}{4}$

   d. $\frac{-3 \pm \sqrt{41}}{4}$

   e. $\frac{3 \pm \sqrt{41}}{4}$

31. Simplify the expression $3q\left(\dfrac{(3q)^4}{3q^{-2}} \right)$.

   a. $81q^3$

   b. $81q^7$

   c. $729q^3$

   d. $729q^7$

   e. $2187q^7$

32. Express $\left(3.14 \times 10^3\right)^3$ in proper scientific notation format.

   a. 3.14×10^6

   b. 3.14×10^9

   c. 3.0959144×10^6

   d. 3.0959144×10^9

   e. 3.0959144×10^{10}

33. A family on vacation drives 123 miles in 2 hours, then gets stuck in traffic and goes 4 miles in the next 15 minutes. The remaining 191 miles of the trip take $3\frac{3}{4}$ hours. What was their average rate of speed to the nearest tenth of a mile per hour?

   a. 15.3 miles per hour

   b. 42.8 miles per hour

   c. 53.0 miles per hour

   d. 53.9 miles per hour

   e. 54.6 miles per hour

34. Which point, when drawn to the origin, forms a line perpendicular to the line formed by the equation $x - 2y = 4$?

    a. (1, 2)
    b. (2, 1)
    c. (-1, 2)
    d. (-2, 1)
    e. (-1,-2)

35. Simplify: $\dfrac{33 + 10i}{2 + 5i}$.

    a. $4 - 5i$
    b. $\dfrac{41}{4+5i}$
    c. $\dfrac{4+5i}{41}$
    d. $5i - 4$
    e. $4 + 5i$

36. Find the value of x if $16^{x-1} = \frac{1}{2}$.

    a. $\frac{1}{4}$
    b. $\frac{3}{4}$
    c. $\frac{1}{2}$
    d. $\frac{3}{2}$
    e. $\frac{9}{16}$

37. What is the value of $\cos\left(\dfrac{3\pi}{2} - \dfrac{\pi}{3}\right)$ if $\cos(\alpha - \beta) = \cos\alpha\cos\beta + \sin\alpha\sin\beta$?

    a. 0
    b. $\frac{1}{2}$
    c. $-\frac{1}{2}$
    d. $\frac{\sqrt{3}}{2}$
    e. $-\frac{\sqrt{3}}{2}$

38. $(a - 2b)^2 - (2ab - 3a^2 - b^2) =$

    a. $4a^2 - 2ab - 3b^2$
    b. $4a^2 - 2ab + 5b^2$
    c. $4a^2 - 6ab + 5b^2$
    d. $-2a^2 - 2ab + 3b^2$
    e. $-2a^2 - 2ab - 5b^2$

39. $\dfrac{5 + 3\sqrt{2}}{5 - 3\sqrt{2}} =$

   a. 2

   b. $\dfrac{7}{43 + 30\sqrt{2}}$

   c. $\dfrac{7}{25 + 39\sqrt{2}}$

   d. $\dfrac{25 + 39\sqrt{2}}{7}$

   e. $\dfrac{43 + 30\sqrt{2}}{7}$

40. Find the value of n if $2n - 7 = 3(n - 2)$.

   a. -13

   b. -5

   c. -1

   d. 1

   e. 5

41. What is the relationship between the lines formed by the equations $7x = 3y - 3$ and $7x = 3 - 3y$?

   I.   They are parallel

   II.   They are perpendicular

   III.   They intersect

   a. I only

   b. II only

   c. III only

   d. II and III

   e. None of the above.

42. What is the sixth term in the geometric sequence 1, -5, 25, -125, . . . ?

   a. 625

   b. -625

   c. 3125

   d. -3125

   e. 15625

43. Simplify the expression $3\log_b p + \frac{1}{2}\log_b q$.

   a. $\log_b p^3 \sqrt{q}$

   b. $\log_b (p^3 + \sqrt{q})$

   c. $\log_b (3p + \frac{1}{2}q)$

   d. $\log_b \frac{3pq}{2}$

   e. $\log_b \frac{p^3 q}{2}$

44. $(3x + 4)(5x - 3) =$

    a. $15x^2 + 11x + 12$

    b. $15x^2 + 11x - 12$

    c. $15x^2 - 11x + 12$

    d. $15x^2 + 29x + 12$

    e. $15x^2 - 29x - 12$

45. Which is the graph of the equation $x = -y^2 + 2$?

    a.

    b.

    c.

    d.

    e.

46. Find the value of b if $\dfrac{5}{b} = 13 - \dfrac{2}{b}$.

a. $\dfrac{3}{13}$

b. $\dfrac{7}{13}$

c. $\dfrac{7}{26}$

d. $\dfrac{13}{3}$

e. $\dfrac{13}{7}$

47. In the figure below, $\angle CAB \cong \angle BCA$, and the marked angle is $125°$. What is the value of x? Note: The figure is not drawn to scale.

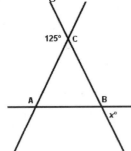

a. 22.5
b. 45
c. 67.5
d. 70
e. 140

48. $\left(\frac{4}{3} \div \frac{1}{3}\right) + \left(\frac{3}{4} \times \frac{2}{3}\right) - \frac{1}{2} =$

a. $\dfrac{1}{4}$
b. 1
c. 2
d. 4
e. 5

49. If $(2x - 7)$ is a factor of $6x^2 - 13x - 28$, what is the other factor?

a. $3x + 4$
b. $3x - 4$
c. $4x + 4$
d. $4x - 4$
e. $4x - 21$

50. A cylindrical oatmeal canister has a diameter of 4 inches and a height of 10 inches. The manufacturing company wants to package the oatmeal in square containers to cut back on wasted storage space. If the new carton has a square base with 4 inch sides, what is the minimum height it must have, to the nearest $\frac{1}{4}$ inch, to hold the same volume of oatmeal? Use 3.14 for the value of π .

    a. $7\frac{3}{4}$ inches
    b. 8 inches
    c. $8\frac{1}{4}$ inches
    d. $8\frac{1}{2}$ inches
    e. $8\frac{3}{4}$ inches

51. A seamstress purchased $5\frac{1}{4}$ yards of fabric to make an outfit. She also purchased $\frac{3}{8}$ of a yard of fabric to make a contrasting collar and cuffs, and $2\frac{1}{2}$ yards of fabric for the lining. How many yards of fabric did the seamstress purchase altogether?

    a. $7\frac{1}{8}$
    b. $7\frac{3}{4}$
    c. $7\frac{5}{8}$
    d. 8
    e. $8\frac{1}{8}$

52. If $\cos\theta = 0$, find all possible values of $\sin\theta$, given $0° \le \theta \le 360°$.

    I.   1
    II. -1
    III. 0
    a. I only
    b. II only
    c. III only
    d. I and II
    e. I, II, and III

53. A bowl fruit is served as part of a breakfast buffet at a conference. There are 21 bananas in the bowl, which is three times as many as the number of oranges. The oranges make up 14% of the total number of pieces of fruit. If each person at the conference was allowed a maximum of 1 piece of fruit, what percentage of the 200 people at the conference could get a piece of fruit from that bowl?

    a. 14%
    b. 25%
    c. 42%
    d. 50%
    e. 56%

54. In the figure below, $\triangle PQR$ is a right triangle; $QR=12$; $QS=3$; $ST=5$' $PR=13$. Find the area of quadrilateral $PSTR$.

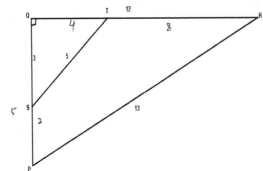

    a. 18
    b. 24
    c. 45
    d. 54
    e. 72

55. $\left(x^{\frac{1}{2}} \right)\left(\sqrt[3]{x} \right) =$

    a. $x^{\frac{1}{5}}$

    b. $x^{\frac{1}{6}}$

    c. $x^{\frac{2}{5}}$

    d. $x^{\frac{3}{2}}$

    e. $x^{\frac{5}{6}}$

56. $\dfrac{15\,p^{6} + 9\,p^{5} - 12\,p^{4} + 6\,p^{3}}{3\,p^{3}} =$

    a. $5p^{3} + 3p^{2} + 4p + 2$
    b. $5p^{3} + 3p^{2} - 4p + 2$
    c. $5p^{9} + 3p^{8} + 4p^{7} + 2p^{6}$
    d. $5p^{9} + 3p^{8} - 4p^{7} + 2p^{6}$
    e. $12p^{3} + 6p^{2} - 15p + 3$

57. If p pounds of ground beef costs d dollars, how many pounds of ground beef can a customer buy with x dollars? Find the general formula that could be used to solve this problem.

   a. $\dfrac{xp}{d}$

   b. $\dfrac{x}{dp}$

   c. $\dfrac{d}{xp}$

   d. $\dfrac{xd}{p}$

   e. $\dfrac{p}{dx}$

58. A student who is $5\frac{3}{4}$ feet tall has a shadow that is 2 feet $10\frac{1}{2}$ inches long. At the same time, a flagpole has a shadow that is $10\frac{1}{2}$ feet long. How tall, to the nearest inch, is the flagpole?

   a. 5 feet 3 inches
   b. 13 feet 3 inches
   c. 13 feet 4 inches
   d. 21 feet 0 inches
   e. 42 feet 0 inches

59. Given matrix $M = \begin{bmatrix} 1 & -3 \\ -5 & 7 \end{bmatrix}$ and matrix $N = \begin{bmatrix} -7 & 5 \\ -3 & 1 \end{bmatrix}$, find the value of M-N.

   a. $\begin{bmatrix} 6 & 8 \\ 8 & -6 \end{bmatrix}$

   b. $\begin{bmatrix} -6 & -8 \\ -8 & 6 \end{bmatrix}$

   c. $\begin{bmatrix} -8 & 8 \\ 2 & -6 \end{bmatrix}$

   d. $\begin{bmatrix} 8 & -8 \\ -2 & 6 \end{bmatrix}$

   e. $\begin{bmatrix} 8 & -8 \\ -8 & 8 \end{bmatrix}$

60. Given circle O with radius 10 in the diagram below, find the length of arc MN.

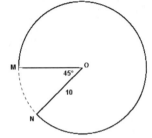

a. 4π

b. 5π

c. $\dfrac{5\pi}{2}$

d. $\dfrac{25\pi}{4}$

e. $\dfrac{25\pi}{8}$

Answer Keys and Explanations

Reading Test

Reading Passage 1

1. B: This question is concerned with the main idea of the passage. Although the passage is not explicit about why Martin and Beth's relationship is strained, by eliminating a number of answer choices, the right answer can easily be found. Choice A can be eliminated because Martin has not lost his job—he receives a page at the end of the passage concerning one of his patients. Choice B is not contradicted by the passage, but all that the reader is told is that Martin and Mary were once together. Choice C can be eliminated because the passage does not indicate how much Martin works. Choice D can be eliminated because Martin tells Beth that if she wants to go to the movies, they can go. Choice E can be eliminated because the passage does not tell the reader how much Beth talks. The best choice, then, is B.

2. C: This question is concerned with the passage's details. Each of the answer choices can initially seem appropriate if the reader reads the passage too quickly or if the reader convinces him or herself that a given choice could be the correct answer. The passage is explicit, however: "She wanted her husband back."

3. E: This question asks for the definition of "fine" within the passage. "Fine" can mean "good," "precious," or "sharp," but this question asks for the meaning of "fine" within the passage itself. Choices A and B are inappropriate because Beth says that "fine" used to mean these things but does not any longer. Choices C and D are inappropriate for the same reason: while "fine" can mean "very good" or "sharp," it does not mean these things within the passage. Choice E is the best answer because Beth says "fine" is "a meaningless word, an excuse not to tell other people what's on your mind." Even though "fine" can mean choices A–D, the question asks what "fine" means according to Beth. Thus, the best choice is E.

4. B: This question asks the reader to make a conclusion based on details from the passage. The reader knows that (1) Martin wears a pager for his job, (2) he has patients, and (3) one of his patients is going into cardiac arrest. Choices A, D, and E can be eliminated because mechanics, film directors, and television producers do not see patients. Choice C seems like a possibility. After all, dentists see patients. Choice B is the best choice because if a person goes into cardiac arrest it is more likely a medical doctor rather than a dentist would be paged.

5. A: This question asks for the best definition of "rapport." A "rapport" is a relationship based on mutual understanding. With this in mind, Choice A might be a good answer, even though it is not an exact match. Choice B can be eliminated because it does not describe a relationship. Choice C can be eliminated because individuals can have a relationship based on mutual understanding without sharing a common goal. Choices D and E can be eliminated because loneliness or boredom have nothing to do with the definition of "rapport."

6. C: This question asks the reader to make an inference about what is going to happen based on the passage. Choice A is inappropriate because the passage says nothing about Martin's level of satisfaction with his job. Choice B is can be eliminated for a similar reason—the passage says nothing about Beth's desire for children. Choice C seems like a good choice because while Martin tells Beth he has to leave to go to work, the structure of the sentence immediately preceding this makes it seem as if Beth knows Martin is going to leave her: "Beth wasn't even sure she knew Martin anymore, but she was confident that it was only a matter of time before everything was not "fine," only a matter of time before he told her..." Choice D is inappropriate because there is nothing in the passage that indicates how long Beth and Martin have known each other. Choice E is inappropriate because the passage explicitly states that Beth had forgiven Martin. The best choice, then, is C.

Reading Passage 2

7. C: With a complex passage like this one, main idea questions may require a re-reading of the relevant portion of the passage because some answer choices may not apply to the question. Answer choice D, for example, is the main idea of the first paragraph, not the second. Answer choices A, B, and E on the other hand, are details that are directly contradicted by the passage. C is the only answer choice that is not contradicted by the passage and applies to the specified paragraph.

8. D: To answer this question, it is helpful to break the word apart. From the passage, it is clear that "to confirm" means "to prove." The prefix "dis" means "not." "Disconfirm," then, loosely means to "not prove." Choice A is inappropriate because it is an antonym. Choice B is inappropriate because "to dissipate" means to break or spread apart. Choice C is inappropriate because "to distill" means to purify or to break down. Choice D is a close match to "not prove". "To disprove" means to prove the opposite of something. Choice E is inappropriate because "forgotten" has nothing to do with confirming or disconfirming.

9. C: Even though this question seems like it requires logical operations, it actually asks for a detail from the passage. Choice A is inappropriate because something that is neither x nor y is irrelevant to the passage. Choice B is inappropriate because something that is both x and y proves the hypothesis. Choice C is a good choice because, using the monkey example, a monkey (x) that has no hair (y) disproves the hypothesis "all monkeys are hairy." Choice D is inappropriate because it is irrelevant to the passage. An example of something that is y but not x could be a hairy llama. Choice E is inappropriate because the passage does not address things that are x, y, and z.

10. D: This is also a detail question. It asks why the author discusses "sample sets." A good answer to this question will say something about probability and/or the size of sample sets. Choice A is inappropriate because the passage does not discuss different monkey species. Choice B is inappropriate because the sample set example shows that it is practically impossible to prove that all monkeys are hairy. Choice C is inappropriate because the passage shows that neither large nor small sample sets can prove hypotheses. Choice D is the best choice because the passage shows that to prove a hypothesis about monkeys, the sample set needed would be functionally too large—every monkey past, present, and future, would have to be examined. Choice E is inappropriate because the passage makes no mention about how different hypotheses compare.

11. D: This question asks the reader to apply information learned in the passage to a new instance. In this case, an eighteen-wheel automobile will lower the probability of the hypothesis "all automobiles have only four wheels." Choices A and C are inappropriate because they refer to proving and disproving and not lowering probability. Choice B is inappropriate because it refers to raising and not lowering probability. Choice E is inappropriate because the passage tells the reader that both confirming and disconfirming evidence does affect the probability of a hypothesis. Choice D is the best answer because an eighteen wheel automobile decreases the probability that all automobiles have only four wheels.

Reading Passage 3

12. A: This question asks for a detail from the passage. According to the passage, Choice A is the only answer choice that is true—in the third paragraph it explicitly says that grieving individuals can be self-destructive. Choice B is not appropriate because the passage does not mention therapy. Choice C is not appropriate because the passage does not discuss complete, or full, healing; it says that the bereaved can begin to heal when they move beyond anger. Choice D is not appropriate because the passage does not mention crying. Choice E is inappropriate because the passage says that anger is both cathartic and therapeutic.

13. E: This question is difficult because the first paragraph of the passage is largely introductory. While the paragraph seems to be concerned with the different stages of the grieving process, these stages serve as context for the main idea of the paragraph: the anger stage of the grieving process is both natural and misunderstood. Choice E is the best choice. Choice A is not discussed in the passage. Choice B is partially contradicted by the first paragraph. Choice C is a detail from paragraph three. Choice D is inappropriate because the relative importance of the stages of the grieving process is not discussed.

14. D: Even if the one does not know the meaning of "cathartic," closely examining the sentence's structure can help determine what the word means. The "in other words" sentence construction alerts the reader that what follows is a restatement of what comes before; thus, "cathartic" and "therapeutic" are related to the phrase "emotional release and allows for the beginning of the healing process." Since something "therapeutic" clearly "allows for the beginning of the healing process," it stands to reason that something "cathartic" is related to "emotional release," which is exactly what answer choice D says.

15. B: Although this question seems to ask for a detail, it actually asks for a larger point from the passage. Choice B is the only good choice because paragraph three discusses how individuals can come to understand how tragedy is generally blameless. Choices A, C, D, and E are all inappropriate because the passage does not address them.

16. D: This question asks for a detail from the passage. Choice A is not a good answer because it is directly contradicted by the passage—anger helps with the grieving process. Choices B and C, while probably true, are not discussed in the passage and so are inappropriate answers. Of course, if choices A, B and C are eliminated, so too is choice E (if even one answer choice is inappropriate, then the answer cannot be "all of the above"). The only remaining choice is D, which is explicitly stated in the fourth paragraph of the passage.

17. D: This question is similar to the previous question. It is a detail question that lists "all of the above" as a possible answer choice. This question differs from the previous one in that it also lists "none of the above" as a possible choice. The passage tells the reader that people who fail to go through the grieving process may experience vague, continued irritability, so answer choice A seems good; accordingly, choice E may be eliminated (if at least one of the choices is a good one, then the answer cannot be "none of the above"). Choice B also looks good because the fourth paragraph explicitly states that such individuals may lose religious faith. Because two answer choices are obviously correct, choice C does not even have to be examined—the correct answer choice must be D, "all of the above."

Reading Passage 4

18. B: Insofar as this is a "purpose" question, the answer should be general in nature. Choice A, while general, is not a good answer choice because this paragraph does not provide contextual information. Choice B is a good choice because the paragraph explains what Descartes means by his proposition and how he arrives at it. Choice C is too specific: "redness" is a detail that helps explain Descartes' argument. Choice D is a poor choice because Descartes is not ridiculed anywhere in the passage. Choice E is inappropriate because it is related to the final paragraph. Choice B is the best answer.

19. C: Although this is a detail question, it asks the reader to draw a conclusion about the author's use of these examples. Choice A is poor choice because the passage makes no judgment on whether these characteristics ultimately exist. Choice B is also a poor choice because the passage does not explore the utility of logic. Choice C is a good choice because the passage is ultimately concerned with demonstrating that only the existence of some object for thinking can be deduced from Descartes' argument. Choice D is inappropriate because the passage does not make any value judgments of physical characteristics. Choice E is inappropriate because the passage does not address quantity or measurement.

20. E: Although this question asks the meaning of a Latin phrase, knowledge of Latin is not needed to answer this question. In the third paragraph, "*cogito ergo sum*" is referred to as Descartes' "proposition." Even if meaning of "proposition" is unclear (it loosely means "thing proposed"), the passage only attributes one saying to Descartes: "I think, therefore, I am." Looking for this statement in the answer choices would thus be the best method for arriving at the right answer, and it is offered word for word in answer choice E.

21. A: These people are mentioned in fourth paragraph. This paragraph mentions "Western Philosophy" and Descartes' "successors," so the answer should be something like "the philosophers who came after Descartes." Choice A is close to this, so this choice should not be eliminated until the other choices are examined. Choice B is inappropriate because "ancestors" are the opposite of "successors." Choices C, D, and E are all poor choices because none of these types of people are mentioned in the passage. So, even though choice A makes no mention of the fact that Hume, Berkeley, and Kant are Descartes successors, it is still the best choice.

22. D: Even thought this question seems as if it asks the reader to draw a conclusion from the passage, it is just a detail question. Choice A is inappropriate because it is directly contradicted by the third paragraph. Choice B is inappropriate because the passage does not explore the relationship between the *cogito* and the external world. Choice C is inappropriate because the passage does not say that color is illusory, but that color must

- 54 -

reside in something. Choice D is explicitly stated in the last sentence of the third paragraph. Choice E contradicts the passage. The best choice, then, is choice D.

23. C: This question asks for the tone of the passage. Choices A and B are inappropriate because the final paragraph emphasizes the importance of Descartes' work. Choices D and E are also inappropriate because the passage points out deficiencies in Descartes' argument. So, the passage both praises and criticizes Descartes' argument. Accordingly, the passage is fair, or balanced. The best answer choice is C.

Reading Passage 5

24. B: This question basically asks for the main idea of the passage as a whole. Choice A is inappropriate because the passage does not discuss automotive stock. Choice B is a good choice because the final sentence of the first paragraph says exactly the same thing. Choice C is not only inappropriate, it is also only true for a very limited number of vehicles. Choice D is so general that it does not really say anything at all. Choice E is irrelevant to the passage. The best choice is, therefore, Choice B.

25. B: Even if the meaning of "detriments" is unclear, the sentence it is used in provides some clues: "While there are many pros and cons associated with automobile ownership, many consumers do not adequately research the specifics benefits and detriments associated with purchasing a particular vehicle." The sentence's structure makes it probable that there is an identification of "pros and cons" with "benefits and detriments." Leaving this aside, if it clear that "pros" and "benefits" are the same thing, then it is likely that "cons" and "detriments" are the same thing. The best answer, then, is B, "Cons."

26. E: This is a detail question with tricky wording in the answer choices. The use of the term "always" should make the reader suspicious. In the real world, things are almost never "always" x or y. For example, choices A and D are explicitly contradicted in the second paragraph. Choice B is doubly inappropriate because of its use of "always" and its irrelevance to the passage (SUVs are not discussed in the passage). While choice C does not use "always," it is not a good choice because the relationship between color and cost is not discussed in the passage. Choice E is supported by the second paragraph and is the best overall choice.

27. E: Insofar as this is an "all of the above question," if the reader can confirm two of the answer choices, he or she need not examine the third. Choice A is a good one because the second paragraph says that the cost of a vehicle is not limited to purchase price alone. Choices B, C, and D are all included in the passage as additional costs of ownership, so since A has already been confirmed, confirming either B, C, or D means that the correct answer is E.

28. B: According to the passage, choice A is inappropriate because if the consumer has done research, he or she will be less likely to be swayed by ancillary concerns. Choice B is explicitly stated in the final paragraph. Choice C is inappropriate because the passage says nothing about the consumer's attitude towards salespeople. Choice D is directly contradicted in the third paragraph. Choice E can be eliminated because choice B is a good answer. Thus, choice B is the best answer.

29. D: This is a difficult question because it is easy to make a simple mistake. The passage explicitly says that choices A and C can be explored on a manufacturer's website. While it seems likely that one could visit a manufacturer's website and find information on a vehicle's color, two things should be noted. First, the passage does not discuss a vehicle's color with reference to a manufacturer's website. Second, the passage does not discuss the relationship between a vehicle's color and its cost. For both of these reasons, choice B is a poor choice; thus, the best answer is choice D.

Reading Passage 6
30. E: Although the passage implies that Bill had not been in school for twenty years, the passage does not say how old Bill is. It might be tempting to try to extrapolate Bill's age from the passage, but this is impossible; in other words, Bill could be forty, fifty, or seventy-five years old (he must be older than twenty because he has not been at school for twenty years), but the passage gives no indication of exactly how old he is. Accordingly, E is the best answer.

31. E: In Bill's exchange with the girl-in-black, the passage shows that Bill is confused. It is also clear that Bill is sad—he misses Martha. The best answer, then, should mention Bill's confusion, his sadness, or both. Choice A mentions neither—this choice says that Bill is bored, or does not care about what is going on. Although Bill is somewhat reflective in the passage, B is not the best choice because it does not capture Bill's general state of mind. Choice C is not appropriate because even though Bill gets offended, he does not really get angry. Choice D is simply ridiculous: Bill is obviously not bursting with joy and energy. Choice E is the best answer because it is directly supported by the passage: Bill can not find the Biology labs, and he cannot understand why the cheerleaders do not thank him for holding the door open.

32. C: Like the first question in this section, it is tempting to tell a story to answer this question. The only information that is provided about Martha in the passage is that she is no longer with Bill. Since the passage says nothing about Martha's infidelity to Bill, choice A is unacceptable. Likewise, choice B may be eliminated because the passage remains noncommittal as to Martha's death. Choice C is a good choice because it succinctly describes Martha's relationship with Bill: she is somehow absent. Choices D and E are not supported by the passage. The best choice is C.

33. A: From the structure of the sentence, it is clear that "dumbfounded" means "could not understand." Choice A is a good choice because "perplexed" is a synonym of confused. Choice B is inappropriate because if something is "rationalized," it is explained or justified. Choice C is inappropriate because "dilapidated" means run-down. To "entreat" means to beg or ask for something; thus, choice D is inappropriate. To "perseverate" means to obsessively focus on something, and while some might think that Bill focuses on rudeness more than is necessary, choice E is inappropriate because within the sentence, "dumbfounded" is used as a synonym of "perplexed." Thus, A is the best choice.

34. C: The passage says nothing about Bill's past profession, so any inferences drawn about his work are in error. Choices A and B are therefore unacceptable. C is a good choice because the final paragraph has a sense of finality about it—Bill is leaving the school, and it is unlikely that he will return. Choice D is not supported by the passage. If Bill misses Martha as much as he says, then it is likely that he really does love her. Even though Bill

- 56 -

cannot find his Biology lab, there is no evidence that he is senile, and so choice E is inappropriate. The best answer is choice C.

Reading Passage 7

35. C: From the sentences preceding the sentence where "diminution" occurs, the reader knows "diminution" must refer to "a process whereby a given liquid is slowly simmered until its volume diminishes." "Diminution" must mean something like "lessening." Choice A is inappropriate because "process" is too general. Choice B is inappropriate because "liquid" would be redundant in the sentence. Choice C captures the idea of "lessening." Although one could make a case for either choice D or choice E, choice C is the best fit with the sentence.

36. D: This question is tricky because a number of the answer choices seem correct but are not supported by the passage. Choice A seems reasonable, but the passage does not say anything about how performing reductions demonstrates skill. Choices B and C also seem reasonable—if reductions are in many dishes, then restaurant customers probably like them, which means that they are popular in contemporary cuisine. However, the passage does not say these things. The passage does explicitly say that many recipes call for reductions, so choice D is a good answer. Since the passage remains silent about hiring practices, choice E can be eliminated. Therefore, D is the best answer.

37. B: This question asks for a specific detail from the passage. Rereading the relevant portion of the passage is thus a wise strategy. Rereading the passage reveals that the chicken is browned and removed, then the butter is added followed by the wine. Turning to the answers, it is obvious that B is the best choice.

38. E: According to the passage, the wine and butter mixture should be reduced by half. After this, chicken stock and chicken breasts should be added. The sauce in this new mixture should be reduced by half. This results in two reductions (A and C in the answer choices). Choice B is not a reduction, according to the passage. The best answer choice is E because it includes the two reductions without mentioning the butter.

39. C: This question initially seems straightforward, but it can be misleading. The inclusion of "all of the above" and "none of the above" as answer choices leads the reader to consider the choices together rather than considering them individually. When the choices are considered individually, it becomes clear that choice A is inappropriate because it contradicts the passage. A common mistake is over boiling, not under boiling. Choice B is likewise contradicted by the passage. Adding butter is part of the chicken Marsala recipe. Since two of the choices have thus far been eliminated, choice D can be eliminated. Choice C is a good answer because the passage describes how adding starches can diminish a sauce's flavor and make it too thick. Since C is a good choice, choice E may be eliminated, which leaves C as the best answer.

40. B: Without looking at the answer choices, a reader may answer this question along the following lines: "the chicken Marsala recipe is an example of a reduction." Choice A seems right, but the importance of reductions is really demonstrated by the first paragraph: reductions are important because they are present in many recipes. Choice B is a close match to "the chicken Marsala recipe is an example of a reduction," and so it is a good preliminary choice. Choice C is inappropriate because it is unclear what a demonstration of

"how not to do a reduction" would consist of. Choice D is obviously incorrect. The reader's experience is not discussed in the passage. Choice E is inappropriate because the author is not mentioned at all in the passage. The best answer is therefore B.

Reading Passage 8

41. E: According to the passage, the exact causes of anxiety are unclear. The question asks for what always causes anxiety. The answer, then, should reflect the fact that there is nothing that always causes anxiety. Choices A and D are inappropriate because the passage does not directly mention genetic or environmental factors, and there is no one thing that always causes anxiety. Choices B and C are inappropriate because both "physiological and psychological factors have been implicated in causing and sustaining anxiety." The best choice is E because the causes of anxiety are not always clear, and they cannot be reduced down to one cause.

42. D: A good definition of "exacerbate" can be found in the first two sentences of the second paragraph. The first sentence says that stimulants make anxiety worse. The second sentence says that these stimulants "exacerbate" anxiety by affecting physical processes in such a manner that anxious individuals might make mistakes about what occurs in their bodies. The definition of "exacerbate" should thus be something like "makes worse." The only answer choice that works with this definition is D.

43. B: According to the second paragraph, "these substances exacerbate anxiety by raising the heartbeat and creating a spike in metabolic processes, and when this occurs, an anxious individual might make a mistaken or exaggerated self-assessment." The answer should say something about how these substances make anxiety worse; they raise metabolic processes, or they may cause mistaken self-assessment. Choice A is inappropriate because the passage says nothing about stimulants calming people down. Choice B is a good answer because it is clearly supported by the passage. Choice C is inappropriate because it is directly contradicted by the passage. Choice D is inappropriate because the passage does not mention anything about heart attacks. Choice E is inappropriate because it is directly contradicted by the passage. The best choice is B.

44. B: Looking at the passage, it seems as if this example serves the purpose of showing how people with anxiety can erroneously blow small events out of proportion. Choice A is inappropriate because the passage does not indicate the boss's gender. Choice B is clearly a good choice. Choice C is a poor choice because it is not supported by the passage. Choice D is inappropriate because this example occurs in a paragraph devoted to psychological not physiological factors. Choice E is inappropriate because the passage does not make any claims about the ability of anxious people to function in the workplace. The best choice is therefore B.

45. C: According to the passage, "reshaping one's perspective can be achieved through psychotherapy or meditation." The correct answer should mention psychotherapy, meditation, or both. Choice A is incorrect because the passage does not mention medication. Accordingly, since one of the answer choices is incorrect, choice D may be eliminated as well. Choice B seems like it could be right, but the passage does not directly mention behavior modification. Choice C is the only answer choice that is directly supported by the passage.

46. D: While it might seem like this question asks the reader to draw a general conclusion about the passage, this question is directly answered in the final paragraph. It is always the best policy to avoid physical exacerbations, but psychological exacerbations should be confronted. Since it is sometimes good to use avoidance, choices A and B are both inappropriate. Choice C is also inappropriate because the passage says that psychological exacerbations should be confronted. Choice D is directly supported by the passage. Choice E is irrelevant because medications are not mentioned in the passage. The best choice is therefore D.

Reading Passage 9

47. C: After asking a series of questions, the first paragraph tells the reader that it is questionable whether there is a difference between human and artificial intelligence. The main idea should somehow be related to this. Choice A is inappropriate because the first paragraph does not make any statements on the actual differences between human and computer intelligence. Choice B is inappropriate because while the paragraph says that there might not be a quantifiable difference between human and artificial intelligence, it does not say that intelligence cannot be measured. Choice C is a paraphrase of the thesis of the first paragraph, and so it is a good choice. Choice D is inappropriate for the same reason as choice A is: the first paragraph makes no judgment on the relative intelligences of humans and computers. Choice E is inappropriate because the first paragraph does not say anything about any type of intelligence being illusory. Choice C is the best answer.

48. D: The Pythagorean theorem example in the second paragraph demonstrates how a computer and a human being both fulfill the definition of intelligence offered in that paragraph. Accordingly, choice A is appropriate because the example shows how human and artificial intelligence operate similarly. Choice B is also appropriate because the paragraph shows how the computer and the human mind each acquire and use the theorem according to the definition of intelligence. Choice C is a poor choice because the example is designed to show how human and artificial intelligence are similar, not different. The best choice, then, is choice D.

49. B: The main idea of the third paragraph should be something like: "insofar as intelligent processes can occur in different physical set-ups, physical characteristics do not seem relevant to intelligence." With this in mind, choice A is inappropriate because this paragraph is not really concerned with "programming"—"programming" is mentioned as a transition to the next paragraph. Choice B is a good choice because it captures the idea that physical characteristics are not really related to intelligence. Choice C is inappropriate because natural selection is not mentioned. Choice D is inappropriate because having a certain physical construction is not a guarantee of intelligence. Choice E is inappropriate because choice B is a good choice. The best answer is B.

50. C: According to the passage, choice A is inappropriate because the passage does not say that being programmed is sufficient for being intelligent. Choice B is inappropriate because it is not supported by the passage. Choice C is a good choice because it is a direct paraphrase of the concluding sentence of the fourth paragraph. Choice D is inappropriate because the passage does not discuss whether or not all humans learn in the same way. Choice E is inappropriate because the passage does not discuss the speeds at which computers or humans learn. The best choice is C.

51. A: Looking over the passage as a whole, it is clear that there are no hard and fast conclusions that are drawn about intelligence and its relationship to humans or computers. The introductory and concluding paragraphs question both how artificial and natural intelligence differ, and the definition of intelligence. The correct answer should somehow refer to this. Choice A is a good answer because it expresses the incertitude of the passage on the difference between human and artificial intelligence. Choice B is inappropriate because the passage clearly contradicts it in a number of places. Choice C is inappropriate because the passage does not argue that computers are intelligent; rather, it argues that they could be intelligent. Choice D is inappropriate because the passage does not question the purpose of intelligence; it questions what intelligence actually consists of. Choice E is inappropriate because the question makes the distinction between "natural" and "artificial" unclear. The best choice is therefore A.

Reading Passage 10

52. C: In general, the first paragraph in an essay (of any length) introduces the discussion at hand or frames a particular debate. Most introductory paragraphs do not introduce extensive content. In this paragraph, there is no clear stance taken on either Buddhist or Western notions of the self, and so choices A and B are inappropriate. Choice C is a good answer because it stresses that the purpose of the first paragraph is to introduce a tension and not to make judgments one way or another. Choices D and E are inappropriate because "egolessness" and "ego-toxicity" are not discussed until the second paragraph. The best choice, then, is C.

53. D: Insofar as this is a definition question, the reader should look back to the passage for the exact wording of the definition. Doing so reveals that choice A is inappropriate because it is explicitly rejected as a valid definition within the passage. Choice B is inappropriate because superego and id are not mentioned within the passage. Choice C is inappropriate because it is the definition for "ego-toxicity." Choice D is a good choice because it is the definition of "egolessness" given in the passage. Choice E is simply a superlative formulation of choice C, and so it is inappropriate. Choice D is the best answer.

54. A: This question is easy to over think. In the second paragraph "egolessness" and "ego-toxicity" are defined and contrasted. The purpose of this paragraph, then, should mention this in some form. Choice A is good because it captures the fact that these terms are distinguished in the paragraph. Choice B is inappropriate because the paragraph only mentions the conflict that Buddhists feel—there is no judgment made on the conflict. Choices C and D are inappropriate because the paragraph does not praise one perspective over another. Choice E is inappropriate because the paragraph does not relate the two perspectives to one another; it simply distinguishes between them. The best answer, then, is A.

55. D: Looking to the passage, it seems as if "*quid pro quo*" means something like "if I do something, then I will be rewarded with something good." Choice A is not a good choice because it says "if I don't do anything, I will get something good." Choice B is inappropriate because money is not mentioned. While choice C might seem like a good choice, the passage does not really talk about what people deserve as much as it talks about what people should do or how they should behave. Choice D is a good choice because "something for something" implies the sort of exchange described in the passage. Choice E is inappropriate because it

- 60 -

essentially says that whatever occurs is what is meant to occur, which is a position not discussed in the passage. Choice D is therefore the best choice.

56. E: This question asks for a detail from the passage, not for a larger, general idea. Choice A is inappropriate because this position describes ego-toxicity, not Buddhist egolessness. Choice B is inappropriate not only because Buddhists do not act out of expectation of reward, but also because the passage does not mention heaven. Choice C is inappropriate because the passage does not address the idea of reincarnation. Choice D is inappropriate because it expresses the same idea as choice A. Choice E is the best choice because in addition to doing good out of compassion, Buddhists do good because it is good for all beings.

Reading Passage 11
57. C: According to the passage, the industry standard growing practices are "buying only shade grown, organic, free trade coffees." Choice A is inappropriate because the passage does not mention manual labor. Choice B is inappropriate because the passage does not mention growing coffee on plantations. Choice C is a good choice because purchasing coffee that is shade grown is explicitly listed as an industry standard. Choice D is inappropriate because the passage does not mention the importance of rainfall to coffee growth. The best choice, then, is C.

58. E: This question can be misleading because the answer is counterintuitive. Choice A is directly supported by the passage, so it seems like a good choice. While choice B seems like a good criterion by which to judge a coffee house, it is not discussed in the passage, and, so, it is not a good choice. Choice C is directly discussed, and it is a good choice. The best choice, accordingly, is choice E: A and C.

59. A: Insofar as the passage is talking about "specialty" coffee, it seems like "specialty" would be a good synonym for "artisanal," and "specialty" coffees are both time and work intensive, according to the passage. Choice A is therefore a good answer because it reflects the fact that specialty coffees have high standards in growing and preparation. Choice B is a poor choice because "artisanal" coffees are premium, not "second-rate." Choice C is inappropriate because nothing in the passage discusses the demand for artisanal coffees. Choice D is inappropriate because even though "artisanal" coffees are expensive, the expense is not related to the definition. Choice E is misleading because "artistic" sounds like "artisanal." The two words are not related in the passage's context, however. The best choice is A.

60. C: The purpose of the passage as a whole can be determined from this passage's introduction: "There are a few simple questions that coffee house patrons should ask to make sure that they are getting the best bean for their buck." To put it another way, the purpose is to convince consumers that they should demand certain standards of the specialty coffee that they purchase. Choice A does not work because the passage does not try to convince people to make coffee at home. Choice B is inappropriate because the passage does not pass judgment on the coffee industry giants (it does not even mention them). Choice C is a good choice because the passage shows consumers which questions to ask to make sure that their coffee houses are abiding by industry standards. Choice D is inappropriate because the passage does not mention reforming the coffee industry. The best answer choice, then, is choice C.

Writing Skills Test

Passage 1

1. E: This is an example of correct use of the possessive. The other answer choices have verbs that do not agree with the subject, are awkwardly constructed, use the possessive form incorrectly or by changing word order make it more difficult to identify the mistake.

2. E: This is an example of agreement. In addition to being a slightly obscure word, "juxtaposition" refers to the relationship between two things, the world's population and the sea. The other answer choices have problems with agreement or punctuation. In answer d there is no need for a parenthetical expression.

3. B: Rising is an intransitive verb that does not take an object. The other answer choices misuse the possessive, use incorrect subject and verb agreement, or use an unnecessary parenthetical expression.

4. E: This is an example of correct agreement between subject and verb. The other answer choices use an unnecessary parenthetical expression, are incorrectly punctuated or misuse the form a noun [relationships].

5. C: This is an example of misusing homonyms, words that sound alike but have different meanings. "Effect" means to bring about a result, while "affect" means to have an influence. The other choices are wrong because of agreement problems in addition to the affect/effect distinction, or are misusing the possessive case.

6. C: This is an example of redundancy as well as wordiness that requires a minimal amount of editing to improve readability and impact. The other choices have agreement problems, are too wordy or too brief. D understates the significance of one of the themes of this essay, the long-term impact of these changes on the environment.

7. B: This is an example of a run-on sentence. All the other answer choices have punctuation problems. Answer choice A lacks punctuation where it is necessary. Choice C has punctuation in the wrong place. Choice D has too much of the wrong punctuation. Choice E omits examples that clarify what the sentences are about. To punctuate this sentence correctly, a student has to understand that the semi-colons are separating the various sentences into units of meaning—large fish, mammals, and small fish.

8. E: This is an example of agreement between verb and subject. To answer it correctly a student would need to know the definition of crustaceans, which is a plural noun, and that "are" is the appropriate verb to agree with this noun. The other answer choices have various agreement problems.

9. C: The other answer choices are sentence fragments [A, B], use faulty punctuation, use unnecessary parenthetical expression [D], or use commas or apostrophes [E] incorrectly. This is a particularly tough problem coming as it does at the end of an already long complicated sentence.

10. D: An adverb is used to modify a number. The other answer choices either use an awkward colloquial form in a formal essay [B], use incorrect punctuation, or use a singular where a plural is required [C].

11. B: The other answers are punctuated with inappropriate or misleading parenthetical expressions [C, D] or use an adverb in place of an adjective [D].

12. E: Among is used when alluding to a group while between is used when discussing two segments. The other choices are incorrectly punctuated.

13. B: "Ecological" is an adjective. It is the science that is concerned with the interrelationships between organisms and the environment. All the other choices use scientific words that sound as if they might fit, but whose meanings are entirely inappropriate.

14. C: This is a homonym problem. A student must know the difference between "weather" which refers to atmospheric conditions and "whether" which is a pronoun or a conjunction. The other answer choices are incorrectly punctuated.

15. E: The first "too" is an adverb modifying late and the second "to" is part of the infinitive "to change". In the other answer choices "to" or "too" are used as prepositions or adverbs—either one or the other or both are wrong.

16. C: All the other answer choices use the possessive or a plural incorrectly.

17. D: This is an unnecessary parenthetical expression. The other answer choices misuse a verb [B] and a plural [B], are incorrectly punctuated [E] or confuse rising with raising [C].

18. C: The adjective "warmer", is used in the comparative form. The other answer choices omit punctuation [B, D] or use the wrong form of "warm" [E].

19. B: All of the other answer choices have misused apostrophes to create an abundance of possessives that make no sense.

20. D: The argument in this essay is focused on the urgency of the environmental problems that are facing our planet and its oceans. This sentence is the culmination of that argument and a call to action.

Passage 2
1. D: This question illustrates ways in which an apostrophe can be misused. Adhesives as a plural might mislead a student to think that 'thing' has to be in the possessive case. Since the first clause in this sentence is an independent clause, a comma is needed to separate it from the subordinate clause introduced by 'so'.

2. A: A paradox [seeming contradiction] describes an adhesive that stick and unsticks. A student who is unaware of the nuances of language or the meaning of words could easily substitute one of the other incorrect choices.

3. C: The misuse of the homonym to, too, and two is common. In this case, the adverbial form used to modify sticky, is the correct form because it means that the glue is not excessively sticky. The other examples are mispunctuated or misuse the homonym.

4. D: This is an exercise in editing. The imprecise and excessive "so to speak" is a colloquial expression that does not fit in almost any context except an attempt to convey a direct quote from a speaker. This is an example of sloppy writing.

5. D: This too is a question about homonyms and the confusion between affect [to influence] and effect [power to influence]. 'Affectively' is an additional distracter because as a variant of affect it deepens the confusion about the correct answer.

6. E: This is a problem in punctuation and whether or not the phrase in question is a parenthetical expression. It is not.

7. D: This is an example of subject verb agreement in which the intervening phrase containing plurals will mislead a student to use "are" instead of "is."

8. A: Each of answer choice is tempting, especially if a student doesn't know the meaning of all the words in the sentence. Choice B is plausible if someone overlooks the use of "finally" in the last paragraph and the abrupt final sentence that ends the essay. C will mislead someone who is confused by the sequence used in the paragraph. D is a poor choice because beginning the essay without explicitly stating the subject would be a weak opening. Choice E is plausible, but the transition from this sentence to what would then be the second line of paragraph 2 is weak.

9. B: A student needs to know the definition of an "artifice." Knowing the difference between an artifice, an artifact (a manufactured object) an artificial quality, and an art form is essential to understanding this segment.

10. E: A semicolon separates two independent clauses. All the other examples misuse commas or create run-on sentences.

11. D: A comma is needed before "but" when introducing a subordinate clause. "But" is needed to make the distinction between sticking and not sticking; hence, "and" will not work in this case.

12. C: Without the semicolon this is a run-on sentence. These run-on sentences are placed together to cause the test taker to question so many of the same mistakes occurring in the same paragraph.

13. D: There is no need for the possessive in this segment. "These" refers collectively to the various kinds of tape that have been created; hence E is in the singular and cannot be correct.

14. B: "Like" is a preposition and is used to make a comparison showing a similarity in degree between things—employees acting as if they were entrepreneurs. "As" is a conjunction. The apostrophes and commas in these choices are distracters.

15. C: The possessive forms in choices D and E are incorrect since "their" refers to the entrepreneurs and not to ideas. Choice A is the contraction for "they are" and is also incorrect.

16. B: The first choice is an example of a dangling modifier. Choices C, D, and E are run-on sentences, mispunctuated or illogical.

17. C: This is another confusing homonym problem compounded by the addition of "were" and "we're."

18. E: The other choices are run-on sentences or mispunctuated sentences. Choice C uses a semi-colon and could end the preceding sentence; however, the next clause should not begin with a capital letter.

19. B: A comma is needed to separate the opening dependent clause from the main clause. The other choices are mispunctuated.

20. C: The final sentence of the paragraph is alludes to all the tapes that were developed as a consequence of Drew's inventiveness. A plural "are" appears in the first clause and is quite deceptive because "none," as in "not one or not any" is the correct noun. Drew is a proper noun and this is another clue to why two of the sentences are incorrect.

Passage 3
1. D: Choices A and B are inverted sentences with inappropriate punctuation. The parenthetical phrase in C doesn't work since it robs an introductory sentence of any significance or link to the paragraph's second sentence. E sounds archaic and contains an inappropriate comma.

2. E: A comma is needed after an introductory verbal phrase. A semi-colon and a period [A and C] are incorrect because there are not two independent clauses. The appositive phrase can't be introduced by an em dash as in D because it is not internally punctuated.

3. A: This looks like a run-on sentence that needs to be divided into two sentences, but it is just long and complex. Choice D looks like a good option too, but the extra comma after "pillaged" eliminates it. All the other choices have commas in the wrong places.

4. C: This is another run-on sentence, but in this segment the possessive case of "lands" in several of the sentences, even the one that is correctly punctuated with a comma, is a subtle distracter.

5. D: The segment contains two homonyms. All of the incorrect choices contain a mistaken combination of the two, or have incorrect punctuation.

6. E: Choices A, B and C do not use correct syntax. Choices C and E confuses "their", "there" and "they're".

7. B: This is an example of the possessive case applied to a plural. Some students might not recognize Spaniard as a singular noun; some will choose D because they will think

'boundless' requires an apostrophe and others will choose C because they don't realize that "s'" is correct.

8. D: The past tense is both precise and correct. The other choices involve auxiliary verbs that do not clarify the time relationship that this essay is describing.

9. D: The word order in this segment is incorrect. Beginning a sentence with a verb is confusing and inappropriate. The punctuation in the other choices is incorrect, even in B, where the word order is correct.

10. B: This is an example of a comma splice. A colon is needed to introduce the fact that dangerous gases were generated. All the other choices are filled with extraneous and incorrect punctuation.

11. B: This segment is a dangling modifier if there is no comma after "despised". The remaining examples are punctuated incorrectly and make little sense as written.

12. E: This is a vocabulary question. One must know the meaning of "indigenous" [native or local] to answer this segment correctly. The other choices starting with "in-" are sure to be confusing.

13. A: "Its" agrees with "population," but the temptation here is to make "place" a plural and overlook the fact that "population" is singular. Choice C substitutes "we're" for "were." Clearly a contraction is inappropriate here, as is the comma in D. Choice E drops the final phrase and creates an incomplete thought.

14. D: The sentence describes the sum of extracted silver: since sentence15 is about the growth of the Potosi through the 18th century, this sentence describes a consequence of that growth and ends with a date from that century. Choice B is illogical since the subject at that point in the essay is the dangerous conditions in the mines. The same holds for choice C. Choice E doesn't work because the context is still Indians, though there is a hint about silver in the reference to pesos.

15. B: The commas bracket a parenthetical phrase. All the other choices have the comma in the wrong place and consequently miss the emphasis in the sentence.

16. E: As it stands, this is a run-on sentence. The semi-colon is one way of making two sentences. A period would do as well, but the comma at the end of choice D is incorrect. The comma at the beginning of choice C creates a parenthetical phrase that makes no sense. Choice B is an incorrect comma splice.

17. D: The antecedent of "it" in the segment is ambiguous, but has to be the Spanish Empire since Spain is in Europe. The careless reader might choose Potosi since it is the subject of the preceding sentence. This reader might also choose E, but it is incorrectly punctuated.

18. D: This segment is an example of a misplaced modifier. The sentence needs to be rewritten so that the thing that threat is describing [piracy] comes immediately after the comma of the introductory descriptive phrase.

19. C: This is an example of parallelism. Choice A is incorrect because the two verbs are not in the same form. Choice B is incorrect because, while the verbs are in the same form, there is no subject. Choice D also lacks a subject and the verbs are not parallel. Choice E changes the sentence to an introductory phrase that does not fit with the rest of the sentence.

20. A: The adjective "its", although it indicates possession, does not require an apostrophe. Choices B and D contain incorrect apostrophes. Choices C and E incorrectly change the singular "its" to plural "their",. In addition, C incorrectly makes an agreement between "ways" and "their."

Math Test

1. B: The amount saved per box of flooring is $\$61.04 - \$27.18 = \$33.86$. To find the number of boxes of flooring the member would have to purchase to save OVER $250, divide $250 by the amount saved per box, or $33.86, and you get $\$250 \div \$33.86 = 7.38$ rounded to the nearest hundredth. Although this number rounds to 7 when you round to the nearest whole number, if the member purchased 7 boxes of flooring, the total savings would be $7 \times \$33.86 = 237.02$, which is not over $250. The member would have to purchase at least 8 boxes of flooring to save over $250. $8 \times \$33.86 = \$270.88$, which clearly meets the requirements of the given conditions.

   **Alternate method: Use each of the choices given and calculate the cost of that number of boxes at each of the two stores. Subtract to find the savings and compare with $250. Beware, however, that four of the five choices will yield a savings of over $250. The problem asks for the MINIMUM number of boxes required to save over $250. Choose the smallest of the four numbers, or 8.

2. E: Because all operations involved are either addition or subtraction, do all calculations in the order they appear in the problem.
$$31 - 27 = 4; 4 + 12 = 16; 16 - 23 = -7; -7 - (-25) = -7 + 25 = 18; 18 + (-6) = 18 - 6 = 12$$
Remember the rule of signed numbers: when you are subtracting a negative number, treat it as if you are adding a positive number. Adding a negative number is the same as subtracting that number. While a group of addends (terms in an addition problem) may be added in any order and still yield the same answer, you must do these in the order given because there is subtraction involved. For example, if you add 27+12 before subtracting from 31, you will get a very different answer!

3. C: Start by converting the percent to a decimal (32% = 0.32) and then continuing with the problem. In word problems, the word "of" is an indication to multiply. In this case, the problem becomes $0.32 \times 750 = 240$. If you remember that a percent is the same as a hundredth, you can read the problem as, "Find 32 hundredths of 750." Written as a decimal, "32 hundredths" is "0.32" and easily translates into the correct format for solving the problem.

4. A: Pay close attention when working with inequalities. Whenever you multiply or divide by a negative number, you must reverse the sign. "Greater than" becomes "less than," and "less than" becomes "greater than." One way to work around this and avoid the confusion is to add and subtract until there are only positive numbers by which you must multiply or divide. In this case, you are asked to solve for x, which is negative. Adding $3x$ to both sides does not change the sign, but it does make x, the term you are looking for, positive: $4 - 3x > 7 \Rightarrow 4 > 3x + 7$. Now you can subtract 7 from both sides to isolate the x-term: $4 > 3x + 7 \Rightarrow 4 - 7 > 3x \Rightarrow -3 > 3x$. Notice that the sign did not change. You subtracted 7 from both sides, but you did not multiply or divide by a negative. To finish solving for x, divide both sides by 3: $\dfrac{-3}{3} > \dfrac{3x}{3} \Rightarrow -1 > x$, which is the same thing as $x < -1$.

5. D: Because the values under the radical signs are different, you cannot combine the radicals. Treat each term separately, and then combine as necessary. Beginning with the first term, $\sqrt[3]{125}$, you should recognize 125 as the product of $5 \times 5 \times 5$. This makes $\sqrt[3]{125}$ =5. Now you have the expression $5 - \sqrt{16}$ and are ready to work with the second term, $\sqrt{16}$. You should recognize this as being equal to 4, making the final expression $5 - 4 = 1$.

6. B: This problem requires you to remember some of the laws of logarithms. The easiest solution is to start with the law $\log_b b = 1$. Therefore, you can rewrite the problem as $2 \log_3 3^2$ so the base in your log is the same as the number following the base. Another law of logarithms important to remember is $\log_b N^E = E \log_b N$. In this problem, as it is currently written, b=3, N=3, and E=2. Using this law of logarithms, you can rewrite it once more as $2 \cdot 2 \log_3 3$. It has already been established that $\log_3 3 = 1$, therefore you are left with $2 \cdot 2 \cdot 1 = 4$. You will get the same answer by starting with the second law we established and writing the problem as $\log_3 9^2$, but you are creating extra work for yourself and adding the risk of making a math error in your efforts to undo what you just did.

7. A: There are two approaches to quickly solve this problem. No matter which method you choose, you need to remember what the "!" means in a problem. The symbol is the factorial symbol, and tells you to multiply the number immediately preceding it by each number from 1 to itself. For example, $5!= 5 \cdot 4 \cdot 3 \cdot 2 \cdot 1 = 120$. If you have a factorial button on your calculator, you can enter the problem as written and your calculator will display the correct answer. The fastest, and easiest, method to solve this without a factorial button is to rewrite the problem as follows: $\dfrac{5!3!}{6!} = \dfrac{5!3!}{6 \cdot 5!}$ You can now cancel the 5! from both the numerator and the denominator, leaving you with $\dfrac{3!}{6} = \dfrac{3 \cdot 2 \cdot 1}{6} = \dfrac{6}{6} = 1$. If you do not see this shortcut, you can always multiply out the numerator and the denominator and divide. It will give you the correct answer, but will take longer.

8. C: You should notice this is a 30-60-90 right triangle. The ratio of the lengths is as follows: Let n represent the short side (the side opposite the $30°$ angle). Then the hypotenuse is $2n$, and the long side (the side opposite the $60°$ angle) is $n\sqrt{3}$. Using this ratio, set 10 (the length of the hypotenuse in the given diagram) equal to $2n$. Therefore, $n = 5$. This is not the answer to the problem. This is the length of the short side. To find x, let $x = n\sqrt{3}$. You already know that $n = 5$, therefore $x = 5\sqrt{3}$.

9. D: The easiest method is to enter the problem in your calculator as it is written. If you are working by hand, set up a long division problem and remember to move the decimal point:

$$1.2\overline{)48} \Rightarrow 12\overline{)480} \Rightarrow 12\overline{)480}^{\,40}$$

10. E: Begin by finding the lowest common denominator of 5 and 4 to get the fractions to have equal denominators. The LCD of 5 and 4 is $5 \times 4 = 20$. Now rewrite each fraction with

the LCD: $\dfrac{2}{5} = \dfrac{2 \times 4}{5 \times 4} = \dfrac{8}{20}$ and $\dfrac{3}{4} = \dfrac{3 \times 5}{4 \times 5} = \dfrac{15}{20}$. Substitute the new fractions in the original

problem and combine like terms: $\dfrac{8}{20} + \dfrac{15}{20} + x = 2 \Rightarrow \dfrac{23}{20} + x = 2$. Write the whole number

as an improper fraction to combine like terms and solve for x:

$$\dfrac{23}{20} + x = \dfrac{2 \times 20}{1 \times 20} \Rightarrow \dfrac{23}{20} + x = \dfrac{40}{20} \Rightarrow x = \dfrac{40 - 23}{20} \Rightarrow x = \dfrac{17}{20}$$

11. B: Begin by factoring the numerator. Assume that $x + 2$ (the denominator) is one of the factors for a quick start to the process. At this point, you should have the following: $2x^2 + x - 6 = (x + 2)(2x - ?)$. The first term of the second set of parentheses must be $2x$ because $2x^2 \div x = 2x$. The sign of the second set must be negative because a positive times a negative equals a negative, and the original problem has -6 as the final term in the numerator. To determine what replaces the "?" above, determine what number multiplied by 2 equals 6. The answer is 3. Now you have fully factored the numerator: $2x^2 + x - 6 = (x + 2)(2x - 3)$. Rewrite the original problem, substituting the factored numerator for the original numerator and solve:

$$\dfrac{2x^2 + x - 6}{x + 2} = \dfrac{(x + 2)(2x - 3)}{x + 2} = 2x - 3$$

12. A: If you rewrite the equation in slope-intercept form, you will know the y-intercept and will be able to quickly eliminate some of the graphs:

$$3x - y = -2 \Rightarrow 3x + 2 = y$$

Now you know that the y-intercept is 2, which is the same as the point (0, 2), and the slope is 3. The only graphs that have the correct y-intercept are A and D. Now look at the slope. Because the slope is positive, the line must go up as it moves from left to right. Only choice A has the correct y-intercept and the correct slope.

13. C: The quadratic formula is $\dfrac{-b \pm \sqrt{b^2 - 4ac}}{2a}$ for all quadratic equations in the form

$ax^2 + bx + c = 0$. In this problem, $a = 3$, $b = -6$, and $c = 2$. Substitute these values in the

quadratic formula: $\dfrac{-(-6) \pm \sqrt{(-6)^2 - 4(3)(2)}}{2(3)}$. Remember that the negative of a negative is

a positive, and that a negative squared is also a positive. Thus,

$$\dfrac{-(-6) \pm \sqrt{(-6)^2 - 4(3)(2)}}{2(3)} = \dfrac{6 \pm \sqrt{36 - 24}}{6} = \dfrac{6 \pm \sqrt{12}}{6}$$. Rewrite 12 as the product of a

perfect square and another number: $\dfrac{6 \pm \sqrt{12}}{6} = \dfrac{6 \pm \sqrt{4 \times 3}}{6}$, then take the square root of 4,

the perfect square, and reduce the fraction: $\dfrac{6 \pm \sqrt{4 \times 3}}{6} = \dfrac{6 \pm 2\sqrt{3}}{6} = \dfrac{3 \pm \sqrt{3}}{3}$

14. D: This problem requires you to remember the fundamental identities of trigonometry. The two that should become obvious in this problem are $\dfrac{\sin \theta}{\cos \theta} = \tan \theta$ and $\sin^2 \theta + \cos^2 \theta = 1$. Substitute these into the original problem and rewrite: $\dfrac{\sin^2 \theta}{\cos^2 \theta} + \sin^2 \theta + \cos^2 \theta = \tan^2 \theta + 1$. By another fundamental identity of trigonometry, $\tan^2 \theta + 1 = \underline{\sec^2 \theta}$.

15. D: There are two approaches to solving this problem. One option is to calculate the value of the numerator and then divide by 27: $\dfrac{\left(3^2\right)^4}{27} = \dfrac{9^4}{27} = \dfrac{6561}{27} = 243$

The second option is to work with the exponents. Change the denominator to a power of 3, and combine the exponents in the numerator: $\dfrac{\left(3^2\right)^4}{27} = \dfrac{3^8}{3^3} = 3^{8-3} = 3^5 = 243$

16. B: Begin by calculating the amount of time the customer rented the truck. If the customer rented the truck at 11:10 a.m., then he had the truck for 50 minutes before noon. If he returned the truck at 1:40 p.m., then he had the truck for 1 hour and 40 minutes after noon, for a total of 2 hours 30 minutes, or 60+60+30=150 minutes. The truck costs $19 for the first 75 minutes, so the customer must pay $19 plus the remaining 150-75=75 minutes. The rental rate is $4.75 for each additional $\frac{1}{4}$ hour, or 15 minutes. 75 minutes is the same as 1 hour 15 minutes, or $\frac{5}{4}$ hours. To calculate the additional charge, multiply $4.75 by 5 (the number of quarter hours of additional time): $4.75 \times 5 = \$23.75$. This is not the answer to the problem! This is only the amount of the charge for the additional time. You must add the initial $19 to get the entire cost of the rental: $19+$23.75=$42.75

17. A: Begin by looking for anything that is common to all three terms. You should notice that each of the coefficients is divisible by three and that each of the x-terms has a power of 2 or more. Factor out a 3 from each term and you have $3\left(4x^4 - 9x^3 + 2x^2\right)$. Next, factor out x^2 from each term and you are left with $3x^2\left(4x^2 - 9x + 2\right)$. The portion inside the parentheses can be further factored as follows: $3x^2\left(4x^2 - 9x + 2\right) = 3x^2\left(4x - 1\right)\left(x - 2\right)$. This step may take a bit of trial and error, but you should be able to find it without too much trouble. Look at the answer choices to get a hint. If a combination you are considering is not a choice, then it is not the correct answer.
If you are having trouble factoring the problem, you can always work backwards. Look at the answer choices and multiply them out to see which one gives the original problem as its answer. This method is more time consuming, but it will yield a correct answer if you get stumped.

18. D: Notice that the x-term has a coefficient of 3 in the top equation and a coefficient of 2 in the bottom equation. The y-term has a coefficient of -1 in the top equation and a coefficient of 3 in the bottom equation. Multiply one or both of the equations by a factor that will yield identical coefficients for one of the terms. In this case, it will be easier to multiply the top equation by 3 to make the y-terms identical:

$$\begin{cases} 3x - y = 10 \\ 2x + 3y = 3 \end{cases} \Rightarrow \begin{cases} 3(3x - y = 10) \\ 2x + 3y = 3 \end{cases} \Rightarrow \begin{cases} 9x - 3y = 30 \\ 2x + 3y = 3 \end{cases}$$

At this point it is crucial to look at the signs associated with the y-terms. The top equation has a negative sign, and the bottom equation has a positive sign. Because the signs are opposite, ADD the two equations together to get a new equation:

$$+\begin{cases} 9x - 3y = 30 \\ 2x + 3y = 3 \end{cases}$$
$$\overline{\qquad 11x + 0y = 33}$$

(Note that if the two signs had been the same (either both positive or both negative) you would have subtracted the equations rather than added.)

Now you can solve for x: $11x = 33 \Rightarrow x = 3$

Do not stop here. To completely solve the system of equations, you must solve for all variables involved. To find the value of y, substitute 3 for x in either of the original equations. It does not matter which equation you choose—you will get the same answer either way:

$3(3) - 3y = 30 \Rightarrow 27 - 3y = 30 \Rightarrow -3y = 3 \Rightarrow y = -1$ or

$2(3) + 3y = 3 \Rightarrow 6 + 3y = 3 \Rightarrow 3y = -3 \Rightarrow y = -1$

The complete solution to the problem is $x = 3$ and $y = -1$, or (3, -1).

If all else fails, you can always substitute the answer choices into the original problem to see which one works.

19. C: The point-slope form of an equation is $(y - y_1) = m(x - x_1)$, given slope m and a point (x_1, y_1). The problem gives the slope $m = -2$ and the point $(x_1, y_1) = (-3, 4)$. Substitute these values into the point-slope form:

$(y - y_1) = m(x - x_1) \Rightarrow (y - 4) = -2(x - (-3))$

Distribute the -2 and combine like terms:

$(y - 4) = -2(x - (-3)) \Rightarrow y - 4 = -2(x + 3) \Rightarrow y - 4 = -2x - 6 \Rightarrow y = -2x - 2$

Do not stop here. While this is a correct equation using the given parameters, it does not satisfy the requirements of the problem. You are told to find the equation in standard form, and you have slope-intercept form. Standard form is $ax + by + c = 0$. Rearrange the terms in your equation to fit this form:

$y = -2x - 2 \Rightarrow 2x + y + 2 = 0$

20. D: This is an order of operations problem. You must remember the correct order of operations: Do all multiplication and division first in the order they appear, followed by all addition and subtraction in the order they appear. The first operator is an addition sign, so skip it and move on to the next one: a division sign. Do this part first.

$6 + 4 \div 2 - 3 = 6 + 2 - 3$. There are no more multiplication or division operators, so go back to the beginning of the problem and do the addition and subtraction in order:

$6 + 2 - 3 = 8 - 3 = 5$

21. A: Remember when dealing with percents that *percent* means *hundredth*. Convert the percent to a decimal $(5\% = 0.05)$ at the very beginning to avoid making the error later.

Now rewrite the formula, substituting the numbers provided in the problem where applicable: $A = P(1 + nr) \Rightarrow A = \$1000\,(1 + 3(0.05))$

Follow the order of operations and solve within the parentheses first:
$A = \$1000\,(1 + 3(0.05)) \Rightarrow A = \$1000\,(1 + 0.15) \Rightarrow A = \$1000\,(1.15)$

Now do the multiplication, and you have the correct answer:
$A = \$1000\,(1.15) \Rightarrow A = \$1150$ If you are still unable to do the problem, look at the answer choices and rule out the obvious wrong answers. Logic will tell you that an account with $1000 at 5% for 3 years is not going to double in those three years. You can eliminate choices C, D, and E. Looking at choices A and B, logic tells us that an account earning 5% is not going to gain half of its original value in 3 years. Eliminate B, and the only answer choice you have left is A.

22. C: When you have two points (x_1, y_1) and (x_2, y_2), the formula for finding the distance d between them is $d = \sqrt{(x_2 - x_1)^2 + (y_2 - y_1)^2}$. Let $(x_1, y_1) = (-3, 4)$ and $(x_2, y_2) = (1, 6)$.

Substituting these values into the formula gives $d = \sqrt{(1 - (-3))^2 + (6 - 4)^2} \Rightarrow d = \sqrt{(1 + 3)^2 + (6 - 4)^2}$. Follow the proper order of operations: parentheses first, followed by exponents.

$d = \sqrt{4^2 + 2^2} \Rightarrow d = \sqrt{16 + 4} \Rightarrow d = \sqrt{20}$. Do not leave your answer in this form. Always check to make sure you have reduced your answer as much as possible. Rewrite 20 as the product of a perfect square and another number:

$d = \sqrt{20} \Rightarrow d = \sqrt{4 \times 5} \Rightarrow d = 2\sqrt{5}$

If you have trouble remembering the distance formula, draw a quick graph of the two points and connect the dots. Treat that line as the hypotenuse of a right triangle and draw the other two sides. You can now tell the length of the other two sides, and then use the Pythagorean formula to get the length of the hypotenuse.

23. D: Begin by simplifying the equation. Divide each term by 2 and you get $2x^2 + 2y^2 = 50 \Rightarrow x^2 + y^2 = 25$. You should recognize this as the equation of a circle whose center is at the origin, and has a radius of 5, because 5 squared is 25. This eliminates choices A, B, and E, because they are not circles. Now look at choices C and D. They both have the origin as the center, so look at the radius. Choice C has a radius of 3.5, and choice D has a radius of 5. The answer is D.

24. E: Substitute $(y - 1)$ everywhere there is an x in the original problem:
$f(x) = 2x^2 - x + 2 \Rightarrow f(y - 1) = 2(y - 1)^2 - (y - 1) + 2$

Squaring the first term gives $f(y - 1) = 2(y^2 - 2y + 1) - (y - 1) + 2$.

Distribute the 2 through the parentheses, combine like terms, and rewrite:
$f(y - 1) = 2y^2 - 4y + 2 - y + 1 + 2 \Rightarrow f(y - 1) = 2y^2 - 5y + 5$

25. B: Cotangent is the reciprocal of tangent, so if $\cot \theta = \frac{3}{4}$, then $\tan \theta = \frac{4}{3}$. You probably remember that $\tan \theta = \frac{\sin \theta}{\cos \theta}$, but don't give in to the temptation to say that $\sin \theta = 4$ and $\cos \theta = 3$. Sine and cosine values are always between 1 and -1, so these numbers fall outside the range of possibilities. To solve this problem, use the trigonometric properties of

- 73 -

right triangles. Sine is equal to $\frac{\text{opposite}}{\text{hypotenuse}}$ and tangent is equal to $\frac{\text{opposite}}{\text{adjacent}}$, so you have a right triangle with sides 4 and 3. Using the Pythagorean formula, you can calculate the length of the hypotenuse: $a^2 + b^2 = c^2 \Rightarrow 4^2 + 3^2 = c^2 \Rightarrow 16 + 9 = c^2 \Rightarrow 25 = c^2 \sqrt{25} = c \Rightarrow c = 5$ You may have recognized this as a 3-4-5 right triangle without using the Pythagorean formula, which would save you the time of doing the calculations. Now you have determined that the opposite side is 4 and the hypotenuse is 5, so $\sin \theta = \frac{4}{5}$.

Even if you are unsure as to how to do this problem, if you remember that sine must be between 1 and -1, you can eliminate choices C, D, and E.

26. C: The quickest way to solve this problem is to cross multiply and divide.
$$\frac{3}{x} = \frac{9}{13} \Rightarrow 3 \times 13 = 9x \Rightarrow 39 = 9x \Rightarrow \frac{39}{9} = x$$
Divide the numerator and the denominator by 3 to reduce the fraction:
$$\frac{39}{9} = x \Rightarrow \frac{13}{3} = x$$

27. D: The problem requires you to remember there are 12 inches in a foot, 5280 feet in a mile, 60 seconds in a minutes, and 60 minutes in an hour. To determine which rate is the fastest, convert them all to the same units. Converting everything to miles per hour will be the easiest. John ran 1 mile in 6 minutes 15 seconds, or 6.25 minutes. To find his speed in miles per hour, divide 60 (the number of minutes in an hour) by 6.25 (the number of minutes it takes him to run a mile): $60 \div 6.25 = 9.6$ miles per hour. To convert Joe's speed, (168 inches per second) to miles per hour, multiply by 60: $168 \times 60 = 10080$ inches per minute, and then multiply by 60 again: $10080 \times 60 = 604{,}800$ .inches per hour. To convert this to feet per hour, divide by 12: $604800 \div 12 = 50{,}400$ feet per hour. To get miles per hour, divide by 5280: $50{,}400 \div 5280 = 9.\overline{54}$ miles per hour. Eliminate Joe as an answer choice. To convert Jim's speed, (875 feet per minute) to feet per hour, multiply by 60: $875 \times 60 = 52{,}500$ feet per hour. To get miles per hour, divide by 5280:

$52500 \div 5280 = 9.943\overline{18}$ miles per hour.
Clearly Jim and Jeremy ran faster than John.

28. B: You are given the values of m and n, so just substitute them in the original problem and solve: $2m^2 + 3mn - 2n^2 = 2(5)^2 + 3(5)(-4) - 2(-4)^2$
Follow the order of operations to finish solving the problem. Solve all exponents before doing any other multiplication: $2(5)^2 + 3(5)(-4) - 2(-4)^2 = 2(25) + 3(5)(-4) - 2(16)$
$$= 50 + 15(-4) - 32 = 50 - 60 - 32 = -42$$

29. A: Rewrite each radical as the product of perfect squares as much as possible:
$$\sqrt{12n^5} - 3n\sqrt{3n^3} = \sqrt{4 \cdot 3 \cdot n^2 \cdot n^2 \cdot n} - 3n\sqrt{3 \cdot n^2 \cdot n}$$

Take the square root of the perfect squares: $2n^2\sqrt{3n} - 3n^2\sqrt{3n}$
Combining like terms gives you $(2n^2 - 3n^2)\sqrt{3n} = -n^2\sqrt{3n}$

30. D: Begin by writing the problem in standard form: $2x^2 + 3x = 4 \Rightarrow 2x^2 + 3x - 4 = 0$
Next, use the quadratic formula to solve for all possible values of x:

$$x = \frac{-b \pm \sqrt{b^2 - 4ac}}{2a}$$ where $a=2$, $b=3$, $c=-4$. Substitute the values into the formula and solve:

$$x = \frac{-b \pm \sqrt{b^2 - 4ac}}{2a} \Rightarrow x = \frac{-3 \pm \sqrt{3^2 - 4(2)(-4)}}{2(2)} \Rightarrow x = \frac{-3 \pm \sqrt{9 + 32}}{4}$$

$$\Rightarrow x = \frac{-3 \pm \sqrt{41}}{4}$$

31. B: Begin by solving the large set of parentheses first. Within the large set of parentheses, do the exponents. Because the number 3 is a constant base throughout the problem, do not worry about multiplying it out at this point: $3q\left(\dfrac{(3q)^4}{3q^{-2}}\right) = 3q\left(\dfrac{3^4 q^4}{3q^{-2}}\right)$

Remember when working with exponents with identical bases in fractions, you can subtract the exponent in the denominator from the exponent in the numerator with the same base. This will eliminate the fraction and make the problem more manageable:

$$3q\left(\frac{3^4 q^4}{3q^{-2}}\right) = 3q\left(3^{4-1} q^{4-(-2)}\right) = 3q\left(3^3 q^6\right)$$

Now multiply $3q$ by the value in the parentheses, adding the exponents:
$$3q\left(3^3 q^6\right) = 3^4 q^7 = 81q^7$$

32. E: Because the parenthetical expression is all multiplication, the exponent applies to each part: $(3.14 \times 10^3)^3 = 3.14^3 \times 10^{3 \times 3} = 3.14^3 \times 10^9$
(Remember that when you are raising an exponent to a power, you multiply the exponents.)
$3.14^3 = 30.959144$ To multiply by a power of 10, move the decimal point to the right the number indicated in the exponent: $30.959144 \times 10^9 = 30,959,144,000$

Written in scientific notation, the number is 3.0959144×10^{10}
Remember that correct scientific notation format has exactly one digit to the left of the decimal point.

33. C: The most efficient way to work this problem is to find the total number of miles driven, the total number of hours driven, and divide to find the miles per hour. The total miles driven are $123 + 4 + 191 = 318$ miles. To find the total number of hours, convert 15 minutes to $\frac{15}{60} = \frac{1}{4}$ hour and add. The total hours driven is $2 + \frac{1}{4} + 3\frac{3}{4} = 6$ hours. To find the average rate of speed for the trip, divide the total miles driven by the total hours driven: $318 \div 6 = 53$ miles per hour.

34. C: Begin by finding the slope of the given line. The easiest way is to rearrange the equation so that it is in slope-intercept form:
$$x - 2y = 4 \Rightarrow x = 2y + 4 \Rightarrow x - 4 = 2y \Rightarrow \tfrac{x}{2} - 2 = y \Rightarrow y = \tfrac{1}{2}x - 2$$
When an equation is in the form $y = mx + b$, m is the slope. In this case, $m = \frac{1}{2}$.

The question asks about a line perpendicular to the given line. Perpendicular lines have slopes that are negative reciprocals of each other. In this case, the given slope is $\frac{1}{2}$, so the slope of a perpendicular line must be $-\frac{2}{1}$ or -2. Look at the answer choices and calculate the slope of each pair of points using the formula $m = \dfrac{y_2 - y_1}{x_2 - x_1}$ for any two given points (x_1, y_1) and (x_2, y_2). You know that the origin (0, 0) is one of the points in each case, so let it represent (x_1, y_1) to make the math easier. Look for the pair that has -2 as the answer. Choice A gives $\frac{2-0}{1-0} = 2$. Choice B gives $\frac{1-0}{2-0} = \frac{1}{2}$. This line is parallel to the given equation, not perpendicular. Choice C gives $\frac{2-0}{-1-0} = \frac{2}{-1} = -2$. Choice D gives $\frac{1-0}{-2-0} = \frac{1}{-2}$. Choice E gives $\frac{-2-0}{-1-0} = \frac{-2}{-1} = 2$. C is the only choice that is perpendicular.

35. A: Begin by rationalizing the denominator. To do this, change the sign of the i-term in the denominator, and multiply the numerator and denominator by the new expression:

$$\frac{33 + 10i}{2 + 5i} \times \frac{2 - 5i}{2 - 5i} = \frac{(33 + 10i)(2 - 5i)}{(2 + 5i)(2 - 5i)} = \frac{66 - 165i + 20i - 50i^2}{4 - 10i + 10i - 25i^2}$$

Remember that i is an imaginary number equal to $\sqrt{-1}$ and that $i^2 = -1$. Make the necessary substitutions in the problem and combine like terms:

$$\frac{66 - 165i + 20i - 50i^2}{4 - 10i + 10i - 25i^2} = \frac{66 - 145i - 50(-1)}{4 - 25(-1)} = \frac{66 - 145i + 50}{4 + 25} = \frac{116 - 145i}{29}$$

Look for ways to reduce the fraction. You should notice that each term is divisible by 29. Divide each term in the numerator and denominator by 29:

$$\frac{116 - 145i}{29} = \frac{29(4) - 29(5)i}{29} = \frac{29(4 - 5i)}{29} = 4 - 5i$$

36. B: You should recognize 16 as the square of 4, and 2 (the denominator in the fraction) as the square root of 4. Rewrite the problem using powers of 4, remembering that the square root of a number is the same as that number raised to the $\frac{1}{2}$ power.

$$16^{x-1} = \frac{1}{2} \Rightarrow (4^2)^{x-1} = \frac{1}{4^{\frac{1}{2}}} \Rightarrow (4^2)^{x-1} = 4^{-\frac{1}{2}} \Rightarrow 4^{2x-2} = 4^{-\frac{1}{2}}$$

Remember that a negative exponent of a whole number or a numerator is equal to the same base in the denominator with a positive exponent.
When the base on both sides of the equal sign is the same, set the exponents equal and solve:

$$4^{2x-2} = 4^{-\frac{1}{2}} \Rightarrow 2x - 2 = -\frac{1}{2} \Rightarrow 2x = 2 - \frac{1}{2} \Rightarrow 2x = \frac{3}{2} \Rightarrow x = \frac{3}{4}$$

Note: This is the same as taking the log of both sides.
When all else fails, you can try substituting the answer choices into the original problem and using your calculator. You will get the right answer, but it may take a while, and you are opening yourself up to errors in entering the information on your calculator.

37. E: Start by finding the sine and cosine of $\frac{3\pi}{2}$ and $\frac{\pi}{3}$. These are common angles represented in radians. $\sin \frac{3\pi}{2} = -1$; $\sin \frac{\pi}{3} = \frac{\sqrt{3}}{2}$; $\cos \frac{3\pi}{2} = 0$; $\cos \frac{\pi}{3} = \frac{1}{2}$

- 76 -

Now substitute the values in the second part of the equation:

$\cos \frac{3\pi}{2} \cos \frac{\pi}{3} + \sin \frac{3\pi}{2} \sin \frac{\pi}{3} = 0(\frac{1}{2}) + (-1)(\frac{\sqrt{3}}{2}) = 0 + (-\frac{\sqrt{3}}{2}) = -\frac{\sqrt{3}}{2}$

38. C: Begin by squaring the first set of parentheses, then combine like terms with the second set:

$(a - 2b)^2 - (2ab - 3a^2 - b^2) = (a^2 - 2ab - 2ab + 4b^2) - (2ab - 3a^2 - b^2)$

$= (a^2 - 4ab + 4b^2) - (2ab - 3a^2 - b^2) = a^2 - 4ab + 4b^2 - 2ab + 3a^2 + b^2$

$= 4a^2 - 6ab + 5b^2$

39. E: Rationalize the denominator. This means multiply both the numerator and the denominator of the original problem by the expression formed by changing the sign in the denominator of the original problem:

$$\frac{5 + 3\sqrt{2}}{5 - 3\sqrt{2}} = \frac{5 + 3\sqrt{2}}{5 - 3\sqrt{2}} \cdot \frac{5 + 3\sqrt{2}}{5 + 3\sqrt{2}} = \frac{25 + 15\sqrt{2} + 15\sqrt{2} + 9\sqrt{4}}{25 + 15\sqrt{2} - 15\sqrt{2} - 9\sqrt{4}}$$

Take the square root of 4 in both the numerator and denominator, and combine like terms:

$$\frac{25 + 15\sqrt{2} + 15\sqrt{2} + 9\sqrt{4}}{25 + 15\sqrt{2} - 15\sqrt{2} - 9\sqrt{4}} = \frac{25 + 30\sqrt{2} + 18}{25 - 18} = \frac{43 + 30\sqrt{2}}{7}$$

40. C: Begin by multiplying everything inside the parentheses on the right side of the equation by 3: $2n - 7 = 3(n - 2) \Rightarrow 2n - 7 = 3n - 6$

Combine like terms and isolate n on one side of the equation:

$2n - 7 = 3n - 6 \Rightarrow 2n - 7 - 2n = 3n - 6 - 2n \Rightarrow -7 = n - 6 \Rightarrow -7 + 6 = n - 6 + 6$

$-1 = n$

If you get stuck on this one, you can always use trial and error. Try each of the answer choices until you find one that works.

41. C: Find the slope of each equation. The easiest way to do this is to convert each equation to slope-intercept form, or $y = mx + b$.

$7x = 3y - 3 \Rightarrow 7x + 3 = 3y \Rightarrow \frac{7}{3}x + 1 = y$ Slope (m) is $\frac{7}{3}$

$7x = 3 - 3y \Rightarrow 3y = 3 - 7x \Rightarrow y = 1 - \frac{7}{3}x \Rightarrow y = -\frac{7}{3}x + 1$ Slope (m) is $-\frac{7}{3}$

Parallel lines have equal slopes. Because $\frac{7}{3} \neq -\frac{7}{3}$, the lines are not parallel.

Perpendicular lines have slopes that are negative reciprocals. The slopes are negatives of each other, but not negative reciprocals. The slope of the second line would have to be $-\frac{3}{7}$ for them to be negative reciprocals. Any two lines in a plane that are not parallel will intersect.

42. D: Before you can tackle this one, you must first notice the pattern. You are told it is a geometric sequence, which means that each term is multiplied by the same number to get the next term. In this case, each term is multiplied by -5. The easiest solution would be to multiply the last term given, which is the fourth term, by -5 twice. This would give you $-125(-5)(-5) = -3125$.

If you remembered the formula for finding the nth term of a geometric sequence, you could also use that, but it might take longer, and give you more risk of error:

$l = ar^{n-1}$, where l is the term for which you are looking, a is the first term, r is the ratio by which each term is multiplied, and n is the number of terms in the sequence. In this case, $a=1$, $r=-5$, and $n=6$. Then, $l = ar^{n-1} \Rightarrow l = 1(-5)^{6-1} \Rightarrow l = (-5)^5 \Rightarrow l = -3125$

43. A: Begin by eliminating the coefficient in front of each log expression. Remember that the coefficient of a log becomes an exponent.

$$3 \log_b p + \tfrac{1}{2} \log_b q = \log_b p^3 + \log_b q^{\frac{1}{2}}$$

Next, combine the two log terms. When two logarithmic expressions with the same base are added together, combine them by keeping the same base and multiplying the remaining part:

$$\log_b p^3 + \log_b q^{\frac{1}{2}} = \log_b p^3 q^{\frac{1}{2}} = \log_b p^3 \sqrt{q}$$

44. B: Use the FOIL method to solve this problem. Multiply the **F**irst term in each set of parentheses, followed by the **O**uter terms, then the **I**nner terms, and finally the **L**ast term in each set of parentheses.

$$(3x+4)(5x-3) = \underset{F}{(3x)(5x)} + \underset{O}{(3x)(-3)} + \underset{I}{(4)(5x)} + \underset{L}{(4)(-3)} = 15x^2 - 9x + 20x - 12$$

Combine like terms to get the final answer: $15x^2 - 9x + 20x - 12 = 15x^2 + 11x - 12$

45. E: An equation that contains both x- and y-terms with exactly one of them squared and the other to the first power is a parabola. (You should remember this from looking at the answer choices.) The question is which direction does the parabola open? Look at the x- and y-terms to see which one is NOT squared. The parabola opens over this axis, and the vertex lies on the same axis. In this problem, the y-term is squared and the x-term is not. Therefore, the parabola opens over the x-axis and has its vertex on the x-axis. You can eliminate choice A. The +2 at the end of the equation lets you know that the vertex is 2 units to the right (positive direction) of the origin. You can eliminate choices B and C with this information. The negative in front of the squared term lets you know that the parabola opens to the left, or the negative direction. Choice E is your answer.

The other way to quickly solve this problem is to plot a few points. You can easily find the x- and y-intercepts. Substituting 0 for y in the problem gives you x=2, or the point (2, 0). This eliminates choices A, B, and C. Substituting 0 for x gives you $0 = -y^2 + 2 \Rightarrow y^2 = 2 \Rightarrow y = \pm\sqrt{2}$. You should notice that choice D does not have any y-intercepts, so you can eliminate that choice. E is the answer.

46. B: You must isolate b to solve for b. The easiest way to accomplish this is to multiply each term by b. This will eliminate the fractions and get just one b-term:

$$\frac{5}{b} = 13 - \frac{2}{b} \Rightarrow b\left(\frac{5}{b}\right) = 13(b) - b\left(\frac{2}{b}\right) \Rightarrow 5 = 13b - 2$$

Add 2 to each side to isolate the b-term, and then divide both sides by 13 to solve:

$$5 = 13b - 2 \Rightarrow 7 = 13b \Rightarrow \frac{7}{13} = b$$

47. D: Begin by finding the measures of the angles inside the triangle. Since all straight angles (straight lines) are $180°$, you can easily find the measure of $\angle BCA$. $180 - 125 = 55$. You are also told that $\angle CAB \cong \angle BCA$, so mark that angle 55 as well. If you remember there are $180°$ in a triangle, you can find the measure of the third angle in the triangle: $180 - 55 - 55 = 70$. Vertical angles are equal, so this is also the value of x.

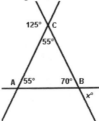

48. D: Solve inside the parentheses first. Remember that when dividing fractions, you invert the second fraction and then multiply:
$$\left(\tfrac{4}{3} \div \tfrac{1}{3}\right) + \left(\tfrac{3}{4} \times \tfrac{2}{3}\right) - \tfrac{1}{2} = \left(\tfrac{4}{3} \times \tfrac{3}{1}\right) + \left(\tfrac{3}{4} \times \tfrac{2}{3}\right) - \tfrac{1}{2} = \left(\tfrac{4\times3}{3\times1}\right) + \left(\tfrac{3\times2}{4\times3}\right) - \tfrac{1}{2}$$
At this point, it is faster to cancel like factors from the numerator and denominator. Notice that there is a 3 in the numerator and denominator of each fraction. Reduce the fractions and solve: $\left(\tfrac{4\times3}{3\times1}\right) + \left(\tfrac{3\times2}{4\times3}\right) - \tfrac{1}{2} = \left(\tfrac{4}{1}\right) + \left(\tfrac{2}{4}\right) - \tfrac{1}{2} = 4 + \tfrac{1}{2} - \tfrac{1}{2} = 4$

49. A: Begin by factoring $6x^2 - 13x - 28$ as you would normally. In this case, you already know one of the factors, so this should make it easier. $6x^2 - 13x - 28 = (2x - 7)(? \pm ?)$ To fill in the first question mark, decide what will multiply by $2x$ to give you $6x^2$. In this case, the term you are looking for is $6x^2 \div 2x = 3x$. Put this in place of the first question mark. $6x^2 - 13x - 28 = (2x - 7)(3x \pm ?)$ Now determine what goes in place of the second question mark. You know the original equation ends with -28, and the factor you are given ends with -7. Divide these number to determine what replaces the second question mark: $-28 \div -7 = +4$. Now you can completely factor the original problem:
$6x^2 - 13x - 28 = (2x - 7)(3x + 4)$

50. B: Start by finding the volume of the existing oatmeal canister. The formula for the volume of a container is to multiply the area of the base times the height. In this case, the base is a circle with diameter of 4. This makes the radius 2, and the area of the base
$$A = \pi r^2 \Rightarrow A = \pi(2^2) \Rightarrow A = 4\pi$$
The height was given as 10, so the total volume of the canister is $4\pi \times 10 = 40\pi$. The area of the base of the new container is $A = s^2 \Rightarrow A = 4^2 \Rightarrow A = 16$. To find the minimum height of the new container, divide the total volume of the original container by the area of the base of the new container. Remember that $\pi = 3.14$ for the purposes of this problem.
$40\pi \div 16 = 40(3.14) \div 16 = 125.6 \div 16 = 7.85$ This is more than $7\tfrac{3}{4}$ but less than 8. The minimum height of the new container is 8.

51. E: Set up an equation using the information provided in the problem: $5\tfrac{1}{4} + \tfrac{3}{8} + 2\tfrac{1}{2} = ?$
Before you can add, you must first make sure all fractions have the same denominator. The lowest common denominator of 4, 8, and 2 is 8. Rewrite the equation using the common

denominator: $5\frac{2}{8} + \frac{3}{8} + 2\frac{4}{8} = ?$ Now add the whole numbers to get the whole number portion of the answer, and add the numerators, keeping the same denominator, to get the fraction portion of the answer: $5 + 2 = 7; \frac{2}{8} + \frac{3}{8} + \frac{4}{8} = \frac{9}{8} \Rightarrow 7\frac{9}{8}$ You should notice that the fraction is an improper fraction, meaning the numerator is greater than the denominator. Convert the improper fraction to a mixed number, and add to the whole number 7 you have already found: $\frac{9}{8} = \frac{8+1}{8} = \frac{8}{8} + \frac{1}{8} = 1\frac{1}{8} \Rightarrow 7 + 1\frac{1}{8} = 8\frac{1}{8}$

52. D: When the cosine of an angle is 0, the angle must be either $90°$ or $270°$. $\sin 90° = 1; \sin 270° = -1$. There is never an instance when both sine and cosine of an angle are 0. Options I and II are true, making D the correct choice.

53. B: First, determine how many pieces of fruit are in the bowl. You know there are 21 bananas, and that there are three times as many bananas as oranges. That means there are 7 oranges. You also know that the 7 oranges make up 14% of the total pieces of fruit in the bowl. Set up an equation to find the total number of pieces of fruit in the bowl: $7 = 14\%(x) \Rightarrow 7 = .14x \Rightarrow 50 = x$. There are 50 pieces of fruit in the bowl. Do not stop here. You were not asked to find the number of pieces of fruit in the bowl, but the percent of people at the conference who could get a piece of fruit from that bowl. You know there are 200 people at the conference. If 50 of them can get a piece of fruit from that bowl, then $\frac{50}{200} = \frac{1}{4}$ of the people can get a piece of fruit from that bowl. Convert the fraction to a percent: $\frac{1}{4} = \frac{25}{100} = 25\%$

54. B: The easiest way to solve this is to find the area of the large triangle and subtract the area of the small triangle. First, find the lengths of the missing sides. Because you are dealing with right triangles, use the Pythagorean theorem. In the smaller triangle, the hypotenuse is 5 and one leg is 3. You should recognize the pattern of the 3-4-5 right triangle to know that the other leg is 4. If not, use $a^2 + b^2 = c^2$, where a=3 and c=5 to get b=4. You should also recognize the larger triangle as a 5-12-13 right triangle. Again, if you do not recognize the pattern, use the Pythagorean theorem. The area of the small triangle is $A = \frac{1}{2}(3)(4) = \frac{1}{2}(12) = 6$ and the area of the large triangle is $A = \frac{1}{2}(5)(12) = \frac{1}{2}(60) = 30$. Therefore, the area of the quadrilateral is 30-6=24.

55. E: Rewrite the problem so both terms are expressed with an exponent:

$$\left(x^{\frac{1}{2}}\right)\left(\sqrt[3]{x}\right) = \left(x^{\frac{1}{2}}\right)\left(x^{\frac{1}{3}}\right)$$

When multiplying like terms with exponents, keep the same base and add the exponents:

$$\left(x^{\frac{1}{2}}\right)\left(x^{\frac{1}{3}}\right) = x^{\left(\frac{1}{2}+\frac{1}{3}\right)}$$

Two fractions must have the same denominator before they can be added. The lowest common denominator for the two fractions here is $2 \times 3 = 6$. Rewrite the problem, using 6 as the denominator in both fractions, then add:

$$x^{\left(\frac{1}{2}+\frac{1}{3}\right)} = x^{\left(\frac{3}{6}+\frac{2}{6}\right)} = x^{\frac{5}{6}}$$

56. B: You should notice that each term in the numerator and denominator is divisible by 3. Factor a 3 out of each term and simplify:

$$\frac{15p^6 + 9p^5 - 12p^4 + 6p^3}{3p^3} = \frac{3(5p^6) + 3(3p^5) + 3(-4p^4) + 3(2p^3)}{3p^3} = \frac{3(5p^6 + 3p^5 - 4p^4 + 2p^3)}{3p^3}$$

$$= \frac{5p^6 + 3p^5 - 4p^4 + 2p^3}{p^3}$$

You should notice that each term has p^3 as well. Remember that when you are dividing with exponents, keep the same base, but subtract the exponent in the denominator from the exponent in the numerator. Now you are left with

$$\frac{p^3(5p^3 + 3p^2 - 4p + 2)}{p^3} = 5p^3 + 3p^2 - 4p + 2$$

57. A: Start by finding a way to represent the cost of one pound of ground beef. If p pounds cost d dollars, than the dollars per pound is $\frac{d}{p}$. To calculate the number of pounds of ground beef a customer can buy with x dollars, divide the dollars the customer has by the cost per pound: $x \div \frac{d}{p}$. Remember that when dividing by a fraction, you must invert the fraction and then multiply to get the answer: $x \div \frac{d}{p} = x \cdot \frac{p}{d} = \frac{xp}{d}$

58. D: First, convert each measurement into inches to make the calculations easier.

$5\frac{3}{4}$ feet $= 5\frac{3}{4} \times 12$ inches $= 69$ inches 2 feet $10\frac{1}{2}$ inches $= 24 + 10\frac{1}{2} = 34\frac{1}{2}$ inches

$10\frac{1}{2}$ feet $= 10\frac{1}{2} \times 12 = 126$ inches

Set up a proportion as follows:

$$\frac{\text{height of student}}{\text{length of student shadow}} = \frac{\text{height of flagpole}}{\text{length of flagpole shadow}}$$

$\frac{69 \text{ inches}}{34.5 \text{ inches}} = \frac{x}{126 \text{ inches}} \Rightarrow 69$ inches $\times 126$ inches $= 34.5$ inches (x)

$8694 = 34.5x \Rightarrow 252$ inches $= x$

To convert this to feet, divide by 12:

$252 \div 12 = 21$ feet.

59. D: To add or subtract matrices, simply add or subtract the values in the corresponding position in the matrix, paying careful attention to the signs of numbers.

$$\begin{bmatrix} 1 & -3 \\ -5 & 7 \end{bmatrix} - \begin{bmatrix} -7 & 5 \\ -3 & 1 \end{bmatrix} = \begin{bmatrix} 1-(-7) & (-3)-5 \\ (-5)-(-3) & 7-1 \end{bmatrix} = \begin{bmatrix} 8 & -8 \\ -2 & 6 \end{bmatrix}$$

60. C: The formula for finding the circumference of a circle is $C = 2\pi r$, where r is the radius of the circle. The circumference of the circle in the problem is $C = 2(\pi)(10) = 20\pi$. The portion of the circle in the arc in question is $\frac{45}{360} = \frac{1}{8}$. Multiply this by the circumference to get the length of the arc in question: $\frac{1}{8} \times 20\pi = \frac{20\pi}{8} = \frac{5\pi}{2}$

Practice Test #2

Practice Questions

Reading Test

Questions 1-6 pertain to the following passage:

Peanut Allergy

Peanut allergy is the most prevalent food allergy in the United States, affecting around one and a half million people, and it is potentially on the rise in children in the United States. While thought to be the most common cause of food-related death, deaths from food allergies are very rare. The allergy typically begins at a very young age and remains present for life for most people. Approximately one-fifth to one-quarter of children with a peanut allergy, however, outgrow it. Treatment involves careful avoidance of peanuts or any food that may contain peanut pieces or oils. For some sufferers, exposure to even the smallest amount of peanut product can trigger a serious reaction.

Symptoms of peanut allergy can include skin reactions, itching around the mouth, digestive problems, shortness of breath, and runny or stuffy nose. The most severe peanut allergies can result in anaphylaxis, which requires immediate treatment with epinephrine. Up to one-third of people with peanut allergies have severe reactions. Without treatment, anaphylactic shock can result in death due to obstruction of the airway, or heart failure. Signs of anaphylaxis include constriction of airways and difficulty breathing, shock, a rapid pulse, and dizziness or lightheadedness.

As of yet, there is no treatment to prevent or cure allergic reactions to peanuts. In May of 2008, however, Duke University Medical Center food allergy experts announced that they expect to offer a treatment for peanut allergies within five years.

Scientists do not know for sure why peanut proteins induce allergic reactions, nor do they know why some people develop peanut allergies while others do not. There is a strong genetic component to allergies: if one of a child's parents has an allergy, the child has an almost 50% chance of developing an allergy. If both parents have an allergy, the odds increase to about 70%.
Someone suffering from a peanut allergy needs to be cautious about the foods he or she eats and the products he or she puts on his or her skin. Common foods that should be checked for peanut content are ground nuts, cereals, granola, grain breads, energy bars, and salad dressings. Store prepared cookies, pastries, and frozen desserts like ice cream can also contain peanuts. Additionally, many cuisines

- 82 -

use peanuts in cooking – watch for peanut content in African, Chinese, Indonesian, Mexican, Thai, and Vietnamese dishes.

Parents of children with peanut allergies should notify key people (child care providers, school personnel, etc.) that their child has a peanut allergy, explain peanut allergy symptoms to them, make sure that the child's epinephrine auto injector is always available, write an action plan of care for their child when he or she has an allergic reaction to peanuts, have their child wear a medical alert bracelet or necklace, and discourage their child from sharing foods.

1. According to the passage, approximately what percentage of people with peanut allergies have severe reactions?
    a. Up to 11%
    b. Up to 22%
    c. Up to 33%
    d. Up to 44%
    e. Up to 55%

2. By what date do Duke University allergy experts expect to offer a treatment for peanut allergies?
    a. 2008
    b. 2009
    c. 2010
    d. 2012
    e. 2013

3. Which of the following is not a type of cuisine the passage suggests often contains peanuts?
    a. African
    b. Italian
    c. Vietnamese
    d. Mexican
    e. Thai

4. Which allergy does the article state is thought to be the most common cause of food-related death?
    a. Peanut
    b. Tree nut
    c. Bee sting
    d. Poison oak
    e. Shellfish

5. It can be inferred from the passage that children with peanut allergies should be discouraged from sharing food because:
    a. Peanut allergies can be contagious.
    b. People suffering from peanut allergies are more susceptible to bad hygiene.
    c. Many foods contain peanut content and it is important to be very careful when you don't know what you're eating.
    d. Scientists don't know why some people develop peanut allergies.
    e. There is no treatment yet to prevent peanut allergies.

6. Which of the following does the passage not state is a sign of anaphylaxis?
   a. constriction of airways
   b. shock
   c. a rapid pulse
   d. dizziness
   e. running or stuffy nose

Questions 7-15 pertain to the following passage:

Daylight Saving Time

Daylight Saving Time (DST) is the practice of changing clocks so that afternoons have more daylight and mornings have less. Clocks are adjusted forward one hour in the spring and one hour backward in the fall. The main purpose of the change is to make better use of daylight.

DST began with the goal of conservation. Benjamin Franklin suggested it as a method of saving on candles. It was used during both World Wars to save energy for military needs. Although DST's potential to save energy was a primary reason behind its implementation, research into its effects on energy conservation are contradictory and unclear.

Beneficiaries of DST include all activities that can benefit from more sunlight after working hours, such as shopping and sports. A 1984 issue of Fortune magazine estimated that a seven-week extension of DST would yield an additional $30 million for 7-Eleven stores. Public safety may be increased by the use of DST: some research suggests that traffic fatalities may be reduced when there is additional afternoon sunlight.

On the other hand, DST complicates timekeeping and some computer systems. Tools with built-in time-keeping functions such as medical devices can be affected negatively. Agricultural and evening entertainment interests have historically opposed DST.

DST can affect health, both positively and negatively. It provides more afternoon sunlight in which to get exercise. It also impacts sunlight exposure; this is good for getting vitamin D, but bad in that it can increase skin cancer risk. DST may also disrupt sleep.

Today, daylight saving time has been adopted by more than one billion people in about 70 countries. DST is generally not observed in countries near the equator because sunrise times do not vary much there. Asia and Africa do not generally observe it. Some countries, such as Brazil, observe it only in some regions.

DST can lead to peculiar situations. One of these occurred in November, 2007 when a woman in North Carolina gave birth to one twin at 1:32 a.m. and, 34 minutes later, to the second twin. Because of DST and the time change at 2:00 a.m., the second twin was officially born at 1:06, 26 minutes earlier than her brother.

7. According to the passage, what is the main purpose of DST?
    a. To increase public safety
    b. To benefit retail businesses
    c. To make better use of daylight
    d. To promote good health
    e. To save on candles

8. Which of the following is not mentioned in the passage as a negative effect of DST?
    a. Energy conservation
    b. Complications with time keeping
    c. Complications with computer systems
    d. Increased skin cancer risk
    e. Sleep disruption

9. The article states that DST involves:
    a. Adjusting clocks forward one hour in the spring and the fall.
    b. Adjusting clocks backward one hour in the spring and the fall.
    c. Adjusting clocks forward in the fall and backward in the spring.
    d. Adjusting clocks forward in the spring and backward in the fall.
    e. None of the above.

10. Which interests have historically opposed DST, according to the passage?
    a. retail businesses and sports
    b. evening entertainment and agriculture
    c. 7-Eleven and health
    d. medical devices and computing
    e. public safety and energy

11. According to the article, increased sunlight exposure:
    a. is only good for health.
    b. is only bad for health.
    c. has no effect on health.
    d. can be both good and bad for health.
    e. has not been studied sufficiently to determine its effect on health.

12. In what region does the article state DST is observed only in some regions?
    a. The equator
    b. Asia
    c. Africa
    d. The United States
    e. Brazil

13. What is an example given in the passage of a peculiar situation that DST has caused?
    a. sleep disruption
    b. driving confusion
    c. twin birth order complications
    d. countries with DST only in certain regions
    e. energy conservation confusion

14. According to the passage, a 1984 magazine article estimated that a seven-week extension of DST would provide 7-Eleven stores with an extra $30 million. Approximately how much extra money is that per week of the extension?
   a. 42,000
   b. 420,000
   c. 4,200,000
   d. 42,000,000
   e. 420,000,000

15. For what purpose did Benjamin Franklin first suggest DST?
   a. to save money for military needs
   b. to save candles
   c. to reduce traffic fatalities
   d. to promote reading
   e. to assist agricultural interests

Questions 16-20 pertain to the following passage:

Sequoia

Most people think that the Giant Sequoia (Sequoiadendron giganteum) is the largest living organism. This conifer grows mostly in groves located in the Sierra Nevada Mountains in California. The biggest single Giant Sequoia is called the General Sherman tree. The General Sherman is 250 feet tall and has a diameter of 24.75 feet at the bottom. The trunk of this massive tree weighs nearly 1400 tons. That's about the weight of 10 trains or 15 fully grown blue whales.

But some people do not think that labeling the Giant Sequoia as the largest living organism is correct. That is because the majority of the material that makes up a tree is made up of dead cells rather than living matter. In addition, there are other types of plants that reproduce in such a way that they are connected with roots under the ground, such as a grove of aspen trees or a field of goldenrod flowers. Some people think that these large, connected groves should be considered the largest organism. In any case, a Giant Sequoia is indeed a massive and beautiful sight to behold indeed.

16. Based on the context of this passage, what is a conifer?
   a. an animal
   b. a tree
   c. a flower
   d. a cell
   e. a plant

17. Is the Giant Sequoia the largest organism?
   a. yes
   b. no
   c. some people think it is
   d. definitely
   e. most people think so

18. What is the General Sherman?
    a. the biggest train
    b. the largest connected organism
    c. the largest Giant Sequoia
    d. a type of whale
    e. a type of cell

19. How many tons is the General Sherman?
    a. 10
    b. 15
    c. 24.75
    d. 250
    e. 1400

20. What is the diameter of the General Sherman tree at the top?
    a. 15 feet
    b. 20 feet
    c. 24.75 feet
    d. 250 feet
    e. This question cannot be answered from the information given.

Questions 21-30 pertain to the following passage:

Ernst Lubitsch

The comedy of manners was a style of film popular in the 1930s. These movies expressed the frustrations of the depression-era poor by mocking the swells of the upper classes, and contrasting their gilded lives to the daily grind of the downtrodden masses. One of the greatest directors of this type of film was Ernst Lubitsch, a German filmmaker who eventually came to Hollywood to make some of his greatest films.

Lubitsch's film career began in the silent era. Born in Berlin, in 1892, he worked at first as an actor, subsequently debuting as a director with the film Passion in 1912. He made more than 40 films in Germany, but the advent of sound brought him to Hollywood, where the new technology was most readily available. After the producer Albert Zukor invited him to come to the U.S. in 1923, he pursued his career in the capital of film until the late 1940s. His signature style – a focus on seemingly insignificant details that imbued them with symbolism in the context of the film – was just as effective in the "talkies" as it had been in silent films. One of his greatest comedies, Trouble in Paradise, starred Herbert Marshall and Miriam Hopkins and was shot in 1932. A stinging social comedy that skewers the illusions of the upper classes, it would not have been well received in his native Germany of the time.

Trouble in Paradise tells the story of a charming, elegant thief. Marshall plays Gaston Monescu, a man whose charm and elegant manners allow him to work his way into the bosom of high society. In the hotels and clubs of the rich, he manages to gain the trust of wealthy individuals until he swindles them. Monescu courts the rich perfume heiress, Mariette, and we are never certain of how sincere his affection for her may be. But he is also in love with his accomplice, Lily, a clever thief in her own right. His eventual decision to leave Mariette for her can be seen as an affirmation of the unity of the working class in this very class-conscious film.

The opening scenes of the film provide a classic example of Lubitsch's wry symbolism. The opening shot is of a garbage can, which is duly picked up by a garbage man and dumped onto what seems to be a truck. But, as the camera pans back, we realize that the truck is, in fact, a gondola, and that the scene takes place in Venice. As the gondolier-garbage man breaks into a romantic song, the camera contrasts the elegant city, its palaces and beautiful canals, with the mundane reality of garbage and necessary, low-wage work.

The film continues to contrast the elegant surfaces of society with the corruption that lies beneath. A classic scene is the first meeting between Monescu and Lily, two thieves with polished manners. In an elegant hotel room, the two engage in a genteel banter filled with seductive double-entendres and urbane banalities. But they are not the baron and countess they profess to be, as their behavior soon makes clear. As the supper progresses, they manage to steal one another's wallets, jewelry, and watches. Finally, they reveal the thefts to one another and sort out their belongings, but Monescu has been won over by Lily's cleverness, for he admires her resourcefulness far more than the undeserved wealth of the upper classes.

Lubitsch went on to make many more films during the 1930s, comedies of manners and musical comedies as well. Among his greatest Hollywood films are Design for Living (1933), The Merry Widow (1934), Ninotchka (1939), and Heaven Can Wait (1943). One of the wittiest directors of all time, he made films in English, German and French, always exhibiting the sharpest eye for detail. His films challenged the intellect of his viewers, and they never disappointed. The juxtaposition of seemingly contradictory elements was always central to his style, as he exposed the falsehoods he found in his world.

21. Which of the following terms would *not* be a good description of Lubitsch's film style, as it is described in the text?
    a. Sophisticated
    b. Erudite
    c. Chic
    d. Boisterous
    e. Highbrow

22. One of the tools that Lubitsch used to mock the upper classes, as shown in the text, was
    a. Lighting.
    b. Talking pictures.
    c. Juxtaposition of contradictory elements.
    d. Urbane banalities.
    e. Music.

23. Lubitsch's signature style can be described as
    a. Double-entendres and urbane banalities.
    b. Using apparently insignificant details as symbols.
    c. Charm and elegant manners.
    d. Corruption underlying high society.
    e. A panoramic of mundane realities

24. Lubitsch first came to the U.S in 1923 because
    a. His films were not well received in Germany.
    b. He was fleeing the Nazi regime.
    c. He was invited by a producer.
    d. He could not make films with sound in Germany.
    e. He wanted to find better scenery for his films.

25. The text tells us that Lubitsch's first film, *Passion* was
    a. An early "talkie."
    b. A comedy of manners.
    c. A film starring Miriam Hopkins.
    d. A failure with the German public.
    e. None of the above.

26. Without considering gender, which two characters have the most in common?
    a. Monescu and Lily
    b. Monescu and Mariette
    c. Lily and Mariette
    d. Monescu and Lubitsch
    e. Lubitsch and Lily

27. The scene with the garbage gondola at the opening of the film shows that
    a. The rich need supporting services.
    b. Venice is kept clean by gondoliers.
    c. Elegance may be only a veneer.
    d. Gondoliers sing romantic ballads.
    e. Lubitsch is a very talented director.

28. Monescu most admires
    a. Lily's wealth.
    b. Lily's cleverness.
    c. Mariette's money.
    d. Venetian gondolas.
    e. His ability to deceive women.

29. In the film, Lily pretends to be
    a. A perfume heiress.
    b. A countess.
    c. A wealthy dowager.
    d. Monescu's partner.
    e. A low-wage worker.

30. In addition to the films he made in Hollywood and Germany, the text suggests that Lubitsch made movies in
   a. England.
   b. France.
   c. Spain.
   d. Lisbon.
   e. Italy.

Questions 31-40 pertain to the following passage:

This Passage Is A Re-Telling Of A Traditional American Indian Legend.
The Black Crow

In ancient times, the people hunted the buffalo on the Great Plains. These huge animals were their source of food and clothing. With stone-tipped spears, they stalked the great beasts through the tall grasses. It was difficult and dangerous work, but they were forced to do it in order to survive.

At that time, there were many crows flying above the plains, as there are today. But unlike the crows we see now, these birds were white. And they were friends to the buffalo, which caused the hunters no end of travail. The white crows flew high above the plains, where they could see all that was happening below. And when they saw that hunters were approaching the herd, they would warn the buffalo. Swooping down low, they would land on the heads of the great beasts and call out to them: "Beware! Beware! Hunters are coming from the south! Caw, caw. Beware!" And the buffalo would stampede, leaving the hunters empty-handed.

This went on for some time, until the people were hungry, and something needed to be done. A council was convened, and the chief of the people spoke to them. "We must capture the chief of the crows, and teach him a lesson, he said. If we can frighten him, he will stop warning the buffalo when our hunters approach, and the other crows will stop as well."

The old chief then brought out a buffalo skin, one with the head and horns still attached. "With this, we can capture the chief of the crows," he said. And he gave the skin to one of the tribe's young braves, a man known as Long Arrow. "Disguise yourself with this, and hide among the buffalo in the herd," the chief told Long Arrow. "Then, when the chief of the crows approaches, you will capture him and bring him back to the tribe."

So Long Arrow donned the buffalo skin disguise and went out onto the plains. Carefully, he approached a large herd of buffalo and mingled among them, pretending to graze upon the grasses. He moved slowly with the herd as they sought fresh food, and he waited for the great white bird that was the chief of the crows.

The other braves made ready for the hunt. They prepared their stone-tipped spears and arrows, and they approached the grazing herd of beasts, hiding in ravines and behind rocks to try to sneak up on them. But the crows, flying high in the sky, saw everything. The chief of the crows saw the men in the ravines and tall grasses, and eventually he came gliding down to warn the buffalo of the approaching hunters.

Hearing the great white crow's warning, the herd ran from the hunters. All stampeded across the plains except Long Arrow, still in his disguise. Seeing that Long Arrow remained, and thinking that he was a buffalo like all the others, the great white crow flew to him and landed upon his head. "Caw, caw. Hunters are approaching! Have you not heard my warning? Why do you remain here?" But as the great bird cried out, Long Arrow reached from under his disguise and grabbed the bird's feet, capturing him. He pushed him into a rawhide bag and brought him back to the tribal council.

The people debated what to do with the chief of the crows. Some wanted to cut his wings, so that he could not fly. Some wanted to kill him, and some wanted to remove his feathers as punishment for making the tribe go hungry. Finally, one brave strode forward in anger, grabbed the rawhide bag that held the bird, and before anyone could prevent it, threw it into the fire.

As the fire burned the rawhide bag, the big bird struggled to escape. Finally, he succeeded in getting out of the bag and managed to fly out of the fire, but his feathers were singed and covered with black soot from the fire. The chief of the crows was no longer white; he was black – as crows are today.

And from that day forward, all crows have been black. And although they fly above the plains and can see all that transpires below, they no longer warn the buffalo that hunters are approaching.

31. According to the passage, the people used stone spears to hunt the buffalo because
    a. They had no metal.
    b. They had no horses.
    c. They needed to eat.
    d. They were plentiful.
    e. They wanted to impress the chief.

32. The word *travail* in the second paragraph means
    a. Travel.
    b. Difficulty.
    c. Anger.
    d. Fear.
    e. Comfort.

33. Which statement best describes what the chief of the crows represents in this passage?
    a. He symbolizes all that is evil.
    b. He is a symbol representing all crows.
    c. He represents the animal kingdom.
    d. He represents other predators that compete with the tribe.
    e. He is a symbol of betrayal.

34. Which of the following best describes the people's motivation for wanting to capture the chief of the crows?
    a. They hated birds.
    b. They wanted to turn him black.
    c. They wanted to eat him.
    d. They were hungry.
    e. They wanted to remove his wings.

35. Long Arrow's activities among the herd while disguised imply that he
    a. Had time to kill.
    b. Wanted to fool the buffalo.
    c. Wanted to fool the crows.
    d. Had forgotten his stone-tipped spear.
    e. Wanted to gain an appreciation for nature.

36. In this tale, the rawhide bag and stone-tipped spears are both details that
    a. Are important for the outcome of the tale.
    b. Paint a picture of the primitive culture of the people.
    c. Make it clear that the people were dependent upon the buffalo.
    d. Show how the people hunted.
    e. Prove the craftsmanship of the people.

37. Why might the chief of the crows have landed upon Long Arrow's head after seeing the other buffalo stampede away?
    a. He thought his warning had not been heard.
    b. He wanted to see the disguise.
    c. He thought that Long Arrow was an injured buffalo.
    d. He had no fear of men.
    e. He needed to rest from a long flight.

38. Once the bird has been caught, what emotions are revealed by the people's deliberations about how to deal with him?
    a. Anger
    b. A calm resolve to change the birds' behavior
    c. A feeling of celebration now that the bird has been caught
    d. Hunger
    e. Jubilation

39. What does the story tell us about why Long Arrow was selected for this task?
    a. He was the bravest man in the tribe.
    b. He was related to the chief.
    c. He was able to act like a buffalo.
    d. The story says nothing about why he was selected.
    e. He wanted to humiliate the chief of the crows.

40. What does this story suggest that the American Indians thought of crows?
    a. They were dirty animals.
    b. They were clever animals.
    c. They were selfish animals.
    d. They disliked the people in the tribe.
    e. They were foolish animals.

Questions 41-50 pertain to the following passage:

This passage is adapted from "Sailing Around the World" by Capt. Joshua Slocum (1899).

I had not been in Buenos Aires for a number of years. The place where I had once landed from packets in a cart was now built up with magnificent docks. Vast fortunes had been spent in remodeling the harbor; London bankers could tell you that. The port captain after assigning the *Spray* a safe berth with his compliments sent me word to call on him for anything I might want while in port and I felt quite sure that his friendship was sincere. The sloop was well cared for at Buenos Aires; her dockage and tonnage dues were all free, and the yachting fraternity of the city welcomed her with a good will. In town, I found things not so greatly changed as about the docks and I soon felt myself more at home.

From Montevideo I had forwarded a letter from Sir Edward Hairby to the owner of the "Standard," Mr. Mulhall, and in reply to it was assured of a warm welcome to the warmest heart, I think, outside of Ireland. Mr. Mulhall, with a prancing team, came down to the docks as soon as the *Spray* was berthed, and would have me go to his house at once, where a room was waiting. And it was New Year's day, 1896. The course of the *Spray* had been followed in the columns of the "Standard."

Mr. Mulhall kindly drove me to see many improvements about the city, and we went in search of some of the old landmarks. The man who sold lemonade on the plaza when first I visited this wonderful city I found selling lemonade still at two cents a glass; he had made a fortune by it. His stock in trade was a wash tub and a neighboring hydrant, a moderate supply of brown sugar, and about six lemons that floated on the sweetened water. The water from time to time was renewed from the friendly pump, but the lemon "went on forever," and all at two cents a glass.

But we looked in vain for the man who once sold whisky and coffins in Buenos Aires; the march of civilization had crushed him -- memory only clung to his name. Enterprising man that he was, I fain would have looked him up. I remember the tiers of whisky barrels, ranged on end, on one side of the store, while on the other side, and divided by a thin partition, were the coffins in the same order, of all sizes and in great numbers. The unique arrangement seemed in order, for as a cask was emptied a coffin might be filled. Besides cheap whisky and many other liquors, he sold "cider" which he manufactured from damaged Malaga raisins. Within the scope of his enterprise was also the sale of mineral waters, not entirely blameless of the germs of disease. This man surely catered to all the tastes, wants, and conditions of his customers.

Farther along in the city, however, survived the good man who wrote on the side of his store, where thoughtful men might read and learn: "This wicked world will be destroyed by a comet! The owner of this store is therefore bound to sell out at any price and avoid the catastrophe." My friend Mr. Mulhall drove me round to view the fearful comet with streaming tail pictured large on the merchant's walls.

41. The passage suggests that the *Spray* was
    a. A packet.
    b. A sailboat.
    c. A bus.
    d. A jet of water.
    e. A port in Buenos Aires.

42. The author found that, since his previous visit, the greatest changes in Buenos Aires had taken place:
    a. Downtown.
    b. At the harbor.
    c. At a lemonade stand.
    d. At the bank.
    e. With the people of the city.

43. The author was shown around Buenos Aires by Mr. Mulhall. How did he come to know Mr. Mulhall?
    a. They had previously met in Ireland.
    b. They had met on the author's first visit to the city.
    c. They met through a letter of introduction.
    d. They met on the docks.
    e. They met downtown.

44. The passage suggests that the "Standard" was
    a. A steam packet.
    b. A sailboat.
    c. A newspaper.
    d. An ocean chart.
    e. A personal journal.

45. The author uses the term "landmarks" to refer to
    a. Monuments.
    b. Merchants.
    c. Banks.
    d. Buildings.
    e. Ports.

46. The passage suggests that the lemonade vendor used fresh lemons
    a. Whenever the flavor got weak.
    b. Every morning.
    c. Almost never.
    d. When he could get them.
    e. When customers made complaints.

47. The meaning of the word "fain" (Paragraph 4) is closest to
   a. Anxiously.
   b. Willingly.
   c. Desperately.
   d. Indifferently.
   e. Possibly.

48. The description of the mineral waters sold by the whiskey merchant (Paragraph 4) suggests that these waters
   a. Could cure disease.
   b. Were held in casks.
   c. Were not very clean.
   d. Were mixed with the cider.
   e. Catered to the taste of anyone.

49. The passage suggests that the merchant with the picture of the comet on his walls had
   a. Malaga raisins.
   b. Been in Buenos Aires when the author first visited.
   c. Painted the sign himself.
   d. Lived for a very long time.
   e. A fascination with astronomy.

50. The sign warning that a comet would cause the end of the world was most likely
   a. An advertising gimmick.
   b. A reflection of the merchant's paranoia.
   c. A way to cover an unsightly wall.
   d. Written about in the "Standard."
   e. A prophetic warning to the people.

Questions 51-60 pertain to the following passage:

Cilia and Flagella

Cilia and flagella are tubular structures found on the surfaces of many animal cells. They are examples of organelles, sub-cellular structures that perform a particular function. By beating against the surrounding medium in a swimming motion, they may endow cells with motility or induce the medium to circulate, as in the case of gills. Ciliated cells typically each contain large numbers of cilia 2 -10 μm (micrometer) long. In contrast, flagellated cells usually have one or two flagella, and the structures can be as long as 200 μm. For both types of structure, the diameters are less than 0.5 μm.

Although they share similar structures, the motion of the two organelles is somewhat different. Flagella beat in a circular, undulating motion that is continuous. The effective stroke of a cilium's beat, which generates the power, is followed by a more languid recovery to the original position. During the recovery stroke, they are brought in close to the membrane of the cell. Cilia usually beat in coordinated waves, so that at any given moment some are in the midst of their power stroke while

- 95 -

others are recovering. This provides for a steady flow of fluid past gill surfaces or the epithelia lining the lungs or digestive tract.

The construction of both organelles is very similar. A portion of the cell membrane appears to be stretched over a framework made of tubulin polymers. A polymer is a long, chain-like molecule made of smaller units that are strung together. In this case, the subunits are molecules of the protein tubulin. The framework, or skeleton, of a cilium or flagellum consists of 9 pairs of tubulin polymers spaced around the periphery, and two more single polymers of tubulin that run along the center of the shaft. This is called a 9+2 pattern.

The motion of the organelles results from chemical reactions that cause the outer polymers to slide past one another. By doing so, they force the overall structure to bend. This is similar to the mechanism of contraction of skeletal muscle. In cilia and flagella, the nine outer polymer pairs of the skeleton have along their lengths molecules of a rod-shaped protein called dynein. The dynein rods can grasp, or bind to, the neighboring tubulin polymer. Energy is then used to drive a chemical reaction that causes the dynein arms to bend, causing one tubulin polymer to move along the length of the other. Through a coordinated series of thousands of such reactions, the cilium or flagellum will beat.

Cilia have also provided some of the best evidence for the inheritance of traits by a mechanism that does not involve DNA. A *Paramecium* is a single-celled ciliated protist that lives in ponds. In one variety, the stroke cycle of the cilia is clockwise (right-handed). In another variety, it is counter-clockwise (left-handed). When the cells divide, left-handed cells give rise to more left-handed cells, and *vice versa*. T.M. Sonneborn of Indiana University managed to cut tiny pieces of cell membrane from a left-handed *Paramecium* and graft them onto a right-handed one. The cell survived, and the direction of the stroke did not change, despite the fact that cilia were now in a cell with a right-handed nucleus and surrounded by right-handed cilia, they continued to rotate to the left. A *paramecium* reproduces by dividing, and Sonneborn followed the transplanted patch for several generations, but it did not change direction. This suggested that the direction of rotation is a property of the cilium itself, and is not influenced by the DNA in the nucleus. In another experiment, Sonneborn transplanted the nucleus of a right-handed cell into a left-handed cell from which the original nucleus had been removed. The cell's cilia kept their counter-clockwise direction of rotation. Further, when this cell divided, all subsequent generations maintained it as well. This proved that the direction of rotation could be inherited in a manner completely independent of the chromosomal DNA.

One theory to explain this is the concept of *nucleation*. According to this idea, the tubulin proteins in left- and right-handed *Paramecia* are the same, so that the genes that give rise to them are also identical. However, once they begin to chain together in a left- or right-handed manner, they continue to do so. Therefore the direction of rotation does not depend upon the genes, but rather on some basal structure that is passed on to the cell's offspring when it divides.

51. Cilia and flagella are both
    a. Proteins.
    b. Sub-cellular structures that perform a particular function.
    c. Organelles that beat in a continuous undulating motion.
    d. Single-celled protists
    e. Cells which are identical in their movement.

52. According to the passage, where would you expect to find cilia?
    a. Stomach lining
    b. Back of the hand
    c. Lining of the heart
    d. Circulatory system
    e. Under a microscope.

53. According to the passage, how many tubulin polymers make up the entire 9+2 pattern seen in cilia and flagella?
    a. 11
    b. 9
    c. 20
    d. 2
    e. Passage doesn't say

54. Two proteins mentioned in this passage are
    a. Tubulin and Paramecium.
    b. Tubulin and dynein.
    c. Tubulin and flagellin.
    d. Tubulin and Sonneborn.
    e. Paramecium and Sonneborn.

55. Which of the following explains how the beating motion of flagella is caused?
    a. The two central polymers slide past one another.
    b. Dynein causes the outer polymer pairs to slide past one another.
    c. Dynein causes each of the outer polymers to bend.
    d. The organelle increases in diameter.
    e. The organelle moves in a circular, undulating motion that is continuous.

56. Polymers are always
    a. Made of protein.
    b. Made of tubulin.
    c. Made of subunits.
    d. Arranged in a 9+2 array.
    e. Found in the epithelia lining the lungs or digestive tract.

57. The passage implies that T.M. Sonneborn was
    a. A zookeeper.
    b. A scientist at Indiana University.
    c. A chemist.
    d. A medical practitioner.
    e. A biologist.

58. It was shown that, if cilia with a counterclockwise rotation are grafted onto a cell whose native cilia beat clockwise, the transplants will
    a. Beat clockwise.
    b. Stop beating.
    c. Beat randomly.
    d. Beat counterclockwise.
    e. Beat for a brief amount of time.

59. The passage describes cilia and flagella and tells us that
    a. Cilia may be 200 μm long.
    b. Flagella are less than 0.5 μm long.
    c. Cells can have more than two flagella.
    d. Flagella are less than 0.5 μm in diameter.
    e. Cilia are more than 0.5 μm in diameter.

60. Sonneborn's experiments showed that
    a. Chromosomes influence the inheritance of rotational direction in cilia.
    b. Rotational direction in cilia is inherited by a mechanism that does not involve DNA.
    c. Chromosomes do not influence the inheritance of rotational direction in flagella.
    d. Rotational direction in cilia is random.
    e. The framework of a cilium or flagellum consists of 9 pairs of tubulin polymers.

Writing Test

The passages below contain several underlined sections, each of which may or may not contain an error of grammar, usage, or style. For each multiple-choice question, the first choice states NO CHANGE. The other choices offer alternatives. Select the best choice from among the five choices offered for each underlined selection.

Passage 1

In 2001, 34% of the population of the United States was overweight. Problems of excessive weight (1)<u>would seem to be</u> associated with the wealth and (2)<u>more than sufficient</u> food supply. (3)<u>Much attention in recent years has been paid</u> to physical fitness and (4)<u>changing their diets</u> to become healthier. It seems logical that, with so much emphasis on health and nutrition, (5)<u>that</u> the solution to our nation's obesity problem would be in (6)<u>sight</u>. However, in a study of a population with moderate food insecurity, it was found that (7)<u>52%</u> were overweight. *Food insecurity* exists when the availability of nutritionally adequate and safe foods or the ability to acquire acceptable foods in socially acceptable ways is limited or uncertain. Over half of (8)the <u>United State's</u> population with a threat of hunger is overweight. Why would obesity be more prevalent among this group of people who have *fewer* resources?

Dieting and surgery do not address the problems of the economic groups with the most severe weight and nutrition problems. Surgery is expensive, and people with limited resources are (9)<u>still</u> not likely to buy expensive health foods when there are cheaper alternatives that satisfy (10)<u>your</u> hunger. The dollar menu at a fast food restaurant is certainly less expensive than preparing a well-balanced meal, (11)<u>and easier too</u>. Another reason for obesity in lower income groups is given by (12)<u>a theory called</u> the paycheck cycle theory. Most paychecks are distributed on a monthly basis, so if a family gets a paycheck, (13)<u>the family</u> will use these resources until they run out. Often money can be depleted before the next distribution. When this happens, there is an involuntary restriction of food. The hypothesis suggests (14)<u>that a</u> cycle of food restriction at the end of the month followed by bingeing that would promote weight gain. The main reasons for obesity and overweight in low-income groups (15)<u>would be</u> periodic food restriction and a poor diet because of financial restrictions.

1.
   a. NO CHANGE
   b. are
   c. seem to be
   d. are not
   e. aren't

2.
a. NO CHANGE
b. more, then sufficient
c. more, than sufficient
d. more-than-sufficient
e. more then sufficient

3.
a. NO CHANGE
b. In recent years, much attention has been paid
c. Much attention, in recent years, has been paid
d. In recent years much attention has been paid
e. Much attention, in recent years has been paid

4.
a. NO CHANGE
b. diet
c. changing diet there
d. changing your diet
e. changing diets

5.
a. NO CHANGE
b. OMIT the word
c. for
d. when
e. because

6.
a. NO CHANGE
b. site
c. cyte
d. cite
e. sites

7.
a. NO CHANGE
b. 52% of them
c. 52% of the population
d. 52% of it
e. 52% of the group

8.
a. NO CHANGE
b. United States's
c. United States
d. United State
e. united states

9.
    a. NO CHANGE
    b. OMIT the word
    c. often
    d. frequently
    e. always

10.
    a. NO CHANGE
    b. OMIT the word
    c. ones
    d. the
    e. all

11.
    a. NO CHANGE
    b. and easier to
    c. and easier two
    d. and easier, too
    e. and easier, to.

12.
    a. NO CHANGE
    b. OMIT the expression
    c. something called
    d. a hypothesis called
    e. a notion called

13.
    a. NO CHANGE
    b. OMIT the expression
    c. they
    d. someone
    e. the families

14.
    a. NO CHANGE
    b. that
    c. that there is a
    d. doing a
    e. to embrace a

15.
    a. NO CHANGE
    b. are
    c. seem to be
    d. come from
    e. will be

Passage 2

Volta Hall is a (1)<u>womens</u> residence located at the western side of campus. It is composed of a (2)<u>porters</u> lodge, a small chapel, a dining hall, a library, a small laundry service, a hair salon, a small (3)<u>convenient</u> store, and three residential buildings designated for students.

Volta Hall (4)<u>has a total</u> of three entry points that provides access to the entire structure. Two of these entries are located on the sides of the dining hall and are left unlocked and unprotected throughout the day. In the evening, usually (5)<u>some time</u> shortly after seven o'clock, these (6)<u>entryways</u> are locked by Volta Hall personnel. This leaves only the main entry, which is located at the front of the hall, (7)<u>as the only way</u> for individuals entering and exiting the hall. No record is kept of students or other persons entering and exiting the building. No identification is required to receive room keys from the porters. Security is so lax that students (8)<u>have been known to even receive</u> more than one room key from the porters and (9)<u>even</u> grab keys from behind the desk without giving notice.

The main entrance is guarded by two porters 24 hours (10)<u>out of each day</u>. The porters are most alert during the morning and early afternoon. During the evening (11)<u>hours</u> and early morning, the porters can be found sleeping. The main entry is usually closed during the late evening and reopened in the morning. Although these doors are closed, individuals have been known to open the latches from the outside, without forcing them, to gain entry.

There are usually additional security guards on the second level. During the day, two security guards are (12)<u>on watch or lack there of</u>. These guards are elderly men who have been known to respond to incidents very slowly, have poor eyesight, are unarmed, (13)<u>and physically out of shape</u>. Throughout the day and most of the evening, these guards can be found asleep at their post. Only one guard is on duty during the evening hours. These men can be found periodically walking around the perimeter of the building "checking" on students. These tactics have been (14)<u>proven to be</u> ineffective (15)<u>toward</u> criminal incidents occurring within the hall.

1.
   a. NO CHANGE
   b. woman's
   c. women's
   d. womens's
   e. womans

2.
   a. NO CHANGE
   b. porter
   c. porter's
   d. porters's
   e. porters'

3.
   a. NO CHANGE
   b. OMIT the word
   c. convenience
   d. connivance
   e. conveniance

4.
   a. NO CHANGE
   b. had a total of
   c. have a total of
   d. had had a total of
   e. will have a total of

5.
   a. NO CHANGE
   b. OMIT the expression
   c. sometimes
   d. a little
   e. almost

6.
   a. NO CHANGE
   b. entry ways
   c. door ways
   d. windows
   e. entriways

7.
   a. NO CHANGE
   b. OMIT phrase
   c. as the way
   d. as the best way
   e. as the better way

8.
   a. NO CHANGE
   b. receive
   c. have even been known to receive
   d. get
   e. recieve

9.
   a. NO CHANGE
   b. OMIT the word
   c. even to
   d. to
   e. even too

10.
    a. NO CHANGE
    b. a day.
    c. at a time.
    d. on their shifts.
    e. out of each and every day.

11.
    a. NO CHANGE
    b. OMIT word
    c. entrance
    d. hour's
    e. hours'

12.
    a. NO CHANGE
    b. on watch or lack thereof.
    c. supposedly on watch.
    d. not enough.
    e. more than enough.

13.
    a. NO CHANGE
    b. and out of shape.
    c. and are physically out of shape.
    d. and are out of shape.
    e. and are out of shape, physically.

14.
    a. NO CHANGE
    b. OMIT the expression
    c. proved to be
    d. tried to be
    e. attempted to be

15.
    a. NO CHANGE
    b. OMIT the word
    c. when it comes to
    d. in curbing
    e. when it came to

Passage 3

Student Log Entry:
This is the first log entry for Mountain Maritime High (1)<u>School's</u> "Student Sailors" program. Our high school mascot is a sea lion, so we call ourselves the "Mountain Lions." We are going out on a university research vessel to collect water from the bottom of the Straits of San Juan.

Our journey began as we cruised over to Victoria on a ferry after a long flight. We were glad that the school paid for all of our transportation because we would have had to (2)<u>have done</u> a lot of car washes to (3)<u>have afforded</u> this trip. (4)<u>At last, we finally</u> boarded our ship on Vancouver Island and got settled in our berths. Soon we met the captain and crew, and (5)<u>soon</u> we were on our way. We sailed for several (6)<u>hours until</u> we arrived at the underwater Axial Volcano on the San Juan Ridge.

When we arrived, the Chief (7)<u>Scientist Dr. Ed Cook and his crew</u> got ready to collect the water samples. Soon, they were ready to cast out (8)<u>this</u> bundle of sampling bottles. The bottles close at any depth so that water can (9)<u>bring</u> back up to the lab. (10)<u>So far we have learned that</u> they are testing the water for trace metals such as iron, manganese, and helium isotopes.

The Axial Volcano erupted in 1998, and these tests (11)<u>will be used to detect</u> what the scientists call magmatic activity . We spoke with a scientist who is filtering the water to find (12)<u>these</u> tiny specks called teps. She thinks they ride up on the hot water plume that moves up from the vents. (13)<u>Last night</u> we were amazed at the marine life that comes up from the depths to see the lights on the (14)<u>ship and all</u>. There are so many marine scientists aboard that we had no trouble finding out (15)<u>what the names are </u>of what we saw.

1.
   a. NO CHANGE
   b. schools
   c. Schools
   d. school's
   e. schools'

2.
   a. NO CHANGE
   b. do
   c. did
   d. have
   e. done

3.
   a. NO CHANGE
   b. have paid for
   c. afford
   d. have done
   e. have afford

4.

    a. NO CHANGE
    b. At last, we
    c. Finally, at last we
    d. We at last
    e. At last, finally, we

5.

    a. NO CHANGE
    b. sooner
    c. then
    d. lately
    e. afterwards

6.

    a. NO CHANGE
    b. hours, until
    c. hours and
    d. hours
    e. hours and hours until

7.

    a. NO CHANGE
    b. Scientist Dr. Ed Cook, and his crew
    c. Scientist, Dr. Ed Cook and his crew
    d. Scientist, Dr. Ed Cook, and his crew
    e. scientist, dr. Ed Cook, and his crew

8.

    a. NO CHANGE
    b. OMIT word
    c. a
    d. some
    e. an

9.

    a. NO CHANGE
    b. brang
    c. be brought
    d. be brung
    e. be broughted

10.

    a. NO CHANGE
    b. OMIT phrase
    c. So far, we have learned that
    d. So far we have learned, that
    e. We have learned, so far that

11.

    a. NO CHANGE

    b. will detect

    c. will look for

    d. will test for

    e. will locate

12.

    a. NO CHANGE

    b. OMIT word

    c. some

    d. any

    e. a few

13.

    a. NO CHANGE

    b. Last night,

    c. START NEW PARAGRAPH

    d. OMIT phrase

    e. In the evening,

14.

    a. NO CHANGE

    b. ship, and all.

    c. ship, and everything

    d. ship.

    e. ship and everything.

15.

    a. NO CHANGE

    b. what are the names

    c. the names

    d. what the names were

    e. the names:

Passage 4

Once upon a time, (1)there was a village in the jungle, a man appeared and announced to the villagers that he would buy monkeys for $10 each.

(2)Seeing as how there were many monkeys around, the villagers went out to the (3)forest, and started catching them. The man bought thousands at $10, (4)and, as the supply started to diminish, the villagers let (5)there efforts lag. The man (6)later announced that he would buy monkeys at $20 each. This renewed the vigor of the (7)villagers and got them catching monkeys again.

Soon the supply diminished even further, and people started going back to their farms. The offer was increased, this time to $25 each, and the supply of monkeys became so (8)few that it was an effort (9)to even see a monkey, (10)let alone catch one!

Well, the man now decided to raise his price (11)again he announced that he would buy monkeys at $50! However, since he had to go to the city on some business, he introduced the villagers to his assistant. "My assistant's name is Eddie. Here he is. (12)This is him. While I am away, Eddie will be the one who buys the monkeys, (13)not me."

With the man gone, Eddie (14)tells the villagers, "Look, I have a great idea. Look at all these monkeys in the big cage that the man has collected. I will sell them to you at $35 and when he gets back from the city, you can easily sell them to him for $50 each."

The villagers all thought this was an excellent idea. They collected their savings, rounded up all the money they could find, and proceeded to buy back all of the monkeys. Eddie took their money and disappeared into the forest. The villagers waited for the first man to return from the city, so they could sell him the monkeys for $50, but he never came. They never again saw him or his assistant, Eddie, (15)only monkeys everywhere!

1.
   a. NO CHANGE
   b. there was once
   c. in
   d. there is
   e. there was at one time

2.
   a. NO CHANGE
   b. Since
   c. Seeing that
   d. Noticing that
   e. Finding

3.
   a. NO CHANGE
   b. forest and
   c. woods, and
   d. woods and
   e. forest; and

4.
   a. NO CHANGE
   b. since
   c. when
   d. but
   e. however

5.
   a. NO CHANGE
   b. OMIT this word
   c. they're
   d. their
   e. they are

6.
   a. NO CHANGE
   b. OMIT this word
   c. soon
   d. kindly
   e. immediately

7.
   a. NO CHANGE
   b. villagers though
   c. townspeople, and
   d. villagers, and
   e. villagers, though

8.
   a. NO CHANGE
   b. OMIT this word
   c. limited
   d. distracted
   e. entangled

9.
   a. NO CHANGE
   b. even to see one
   c. to see even one
   d. to see one
   e. to even glimpse one

10.
   a. NO CHANGE
   b. not only catch one
   c. let alone to catch one
   d. if only to catch one
   e. or catch one

11.
   a. NO CHANGE
   b. again; he announced
   c. again, he announced
   d. again...he announced
   e. again: he announced

12.
    a. NO CHANGE
    b. This is Eddie.
    c. This is Ed.
    d. This is he.
    e. This is Edward.

13.
    a. NO CHANGE
    b. not I."
    c. despite me.
    d. with me."
    e. ;not me.

14.
    a. NO CHANGE
    b. speaks to
    c. told
    d. went to
    e. teld

15.
    a. NO CHANGE
    b. instead of them they saw monkeys
    c. because of the monkeys
    d. so they looked at the monkeys
    e. due to the monkeys

Math Test

1. A box of laundry detergent contains 16.5 oz of product. What is the maximum number of loads that can be washed if each load requires a minimum of ¾ oz of detergent?
   - a. 10
   - b. 50
   - c. 22
   - d. 18
   - e. 16.5

2. Which of the following can be divided by 3, with no remainder?
   - a. 2018
   - b. 46
   - c. 8912
   - d. 555
   - e. 739

3. A bullet travels at 5×10^6 feet per hour. If it strikes its target in 2×10^{-4} hours, how far has it traveled?
   - a. 50 feet
   - b. 25 feet
   - c. 100 feet
   - d. 1000 feet
   - e. 200 feet

4. A blouse normally sells for $138, but is on sale for 25% off. What is the cost of the blouse?
   - a. $67
   - b. $103.50
   - c. $34.50
   - d. $113
   - e. $125

5. Which number equals 2^{-3}?
   - a. ½
   - b. ¼
   - c. 1/8
   - d. 1/16
   - e. 1/12

6. A crane raises one end of a 3300 lb steel beam. The other end rests upon the ground. If the crane supports 30% of the beam's weight, how many pounds does it support?
   - a. 330 lbs
   - b. 990 lbs
   - c. 700 lbs
   - d. 1100 lbs
   - e. 2310 lbs

7. What is the average of $\frac{7}{5}$ and 1.4 ?

    a. 5.4
    b. 1.4
    c. 2.4
    d. 7.4
    e. None of these

8. Which of the following expressions is equivalent to $(3x^{-2})^3$?

    a. $9x^{-6}$
    b. $9x^{-8}$
    c. $27x^{-8}$
    d. $27x^{-4}$
    e. $27x^{-6}$

9. To determine a student's grade, a teacher throws out the lowest grade obtained on 5 tests, averages the remaining grades, and round up to the nearest integer. If Betty scored 72, 75, 88, 86, and 90 on her tests, what grade will she receive?

    a. 68
    b. 85
    c. 88
    d. 84.8
    e. 84

10. A rock group with 5 musicians gets 25% of the gross sales of their new album, but they have to give their agent 15% of their share. If the album grosses $20,000,000, what is each band member's share?

    a. $850,000
    b. $4,000,000
    c. $1,150,000
    d. $650,000
    e. $800,000

11. In a particle accelerator, a neutrino travels in a straight line at a velocity of 1×10^6 meters per second. If it travels for 3×10^{-11} seconds, what is the distance traveled?

    a. 0.3×10^{-5} meters
    b. 3×10^{-5} meters
    c. 0.3×10^5 meters
    d. 3×10^5 meters
    e. 0.33×10^5 meters

12. The weight in pounds of five students is 112, 112, 116, 133, 145. What is the median weight of the group?
  a. 123.6
  b. 116
  c. 112
  d. 118.5
  e. 140

13. Which of the following expressions is equivalent to $(a)(a)(a)(a)(a)$ for all values of a, positive or negative?
  a. $5a$
  b. a^{-5}
  c. $a^{-\frac{1}{5}}$
  d. a^5
  e. $5a^{\frac{1}{5}}$

14. Which value is equivalent to 7.5×10^{-4}?
  a. 0.075
  b. 0.00075
  c. 0.0075
  d. 0.75
  e. 0.0030

15. Which of the following numbers is a prime number?
  a. 15
  b. 11
  c. 33
  d. 4
  e. 88

16. Of the following expressions, which is equal to $6\sqrt{10}$?
  a. 36
  b. $\sqrt{600}$
  c. $\sqrt{360}$
  d. $\sqrt{6}$
  e. $10\sqrt{6}$

17. There are n musicians in a marching band. All play either a drum or a brass instrument. If p represents the fraction of musicians playing drums, how many play a brass instrument?
  a. $pn - 1$
  b. $p(n - 1)$
  c. $(p - 1)n$
  d. $(p + 1)n$
  e. $(1 - p)n$

18. If the two lines $2x + y = 0$ and $y = 3$ are plotted on a typical xy coordinate grid, at which point will they intersect?

    a. -1.5, 3
    b. 1.5, 3
    c. -1.5, 0
    d. 4,1
    e. 4.5, 1

19. Which of the following equations describes a line that is parallel to the x-axis?

    a. $y = 3$
    b. $y = 2x$
    c. $(x + y) = 0$
    d. $y = -3x$
    e. None of the above

20. A straight line with slope +4 is plotted on a standard Cartesian (xy) coordinate system so that it intersects the y-axis at a value of $y = 1$. Which of the following points will the line pass through?

    a. (2,9)
    b. (0,-1)
    c. (0,0)
    d. (4,1)
    e. (1,4)

21. $|7 - 5| - |5 - 7| = ?$

    a. 0
    b. 4
    c. 2
    d. -2
    e. -4

22. Which of the following expressions is equivalent to the equation? $3x^2 + 4x - 15$?

    a. $(x - 3)(x + 5)$
    b. $(x + 5)(3 + x^2)$
    c. $x(3x + 4 - 15)$
    d. $(3x^2 + 5)(x - 5)$
    e. $(x + 3)(3x - 5)$

23. Which of the following expressions is equivalent to $3(\dfrac{6x - 3}{3}) - 3(9x + 9)$?

    a. $-3(7x + 10)$
    b. -3x +6
    c. $(x + 3)(x - 3)$
    d. $3x^2 - 9$
    e. $15x - 9$

24. Evaluate the expression $(x - 2y)^2$ where x = 3 and y = 2.

    a. -1

    b. +1

    c. +4

    d. -2

    e. -3

25. Bob decides to go into business selling lemonade. He buys a wooden stand for $45 and sets it up outside his house. He figures that the cost of lemons, sugar, and paper cups for each glass of lemonade sold will be 10¢. Which of these expressions describes his cost for making *g* glasses of lemonade?

    a. $\$45 + \$0.1 \times g$

    b. $\$44.90 \times g$

    c. $\$44.90 \times g + 10$ ¢

    d. $90

    e. $45.10

26. There is a big sale on at the clothing store on Main Street. Everything is marked down by 33% from the original price, *p*. Which of the following expressions describes the sale price, *S*, to be paid for any item?

    a. $S = p - 0.33$

    b. $S = p - 0.33\,p$

    c. $S = 0.33\,p$

    d. $S = 0.33(1 - p)$

    e. $S = p + 0.33\,p$

27. How many real-number solutions exist for the equation $x^2 + 1 = 0$?

    a. 0

    b. 1

    c. 2

    d. 3

    e. 4

28. Given the equation $\dfrac{3}{y - 5} = \dfrac{15}{y + 4}$, what is the value of *y*?

    a. 45

    b. 54

    c. $\dfrac{29}{4}$

    d. $\dfrac{4}{29}$

    e. $\dfrac{4}{45}$

29. Sally wants to buy a used truck for her delivery business. Truck A is priced at $450 and gets 25 miles per gallon. Truck B costs $650 and gets 35 miles per gallon. If gasoline costs $4 per gallon, how many miles must Sally drive to make truck B the better buy?

    a. 600
    b. 7500
    c. 340
    d. 740
    e. 1600

30. Prizes are to be awarded to the best pupils in each class of an elementary school. The number of students in each grade is shown in the table, and the school principal wants the number of prizes awarded in each grade to be proportional to the number of students. If there are twenty prizes, how many should go to fifth grade students?

Grade	1	2	3	4	5
Students	35	38	38	33	36

    a. 5
    b. 4
    c. 7
    d. 3
    e. 2

31.

y	-4	31	4	68	12
x	-2	3	0	4	2

Which of the following equations satisfies the five sets of numbers shown in the above table?

    a. $y = 2x^2 + 7$
    b. $y = x^3 + 4$
    c. $y = 2x$
    d. $y = 3x + 1$
    e. $y = 6x$

32. A function $f(x)$ is defined by $f(x) = 2x^2 + 7$. What is the value of $2f(x) - 3$?

    a. $4x^2 + 11$
    b. $4x^4 + 11$
    c. $x^2 + 11$
    d. $4x^2 + 14$
    e. $2x^2 + 14$

33. If p and n are positive consecutive integers such that $p > n$, and $p + n = 15$, what is the value of n?

  a. 5
  b. 6
  c. 7
  d. 8
  e. 9

34. In a rectangular x,y coordinate system, what is the intersection of two lines formed by the equations $y = 2x + 3$ and $y = x - 5$?

  a. (5, 3)
  b. (8, 13)
  c. (-4, 13)
  d. (-8, -13)
  e. (2, -7)

35. A package is dropped from an airplane. The height of the package at anytime t is described by the equation:

$$y(t) = -\frac{1}{2}at^2 + v_o + h_o$$

where y is the height, h_o is the original height, or the altitude from which it was dropped, a is the acceleration due to gravity, v_o is the original velocity and t is the time. The value of a is 32 ft/sec². If the airplane is flying at 30,000 feet, what is the altitude of the package 15 seconds after it is dropped?

  a. 29,520 ft
  b. 26,400 ft
  c. 22,800 ft
  d. 0 ft
  e. 300 ft

36. Which of the following could be a graph of the function $y = \dfrac{1}{x}$?

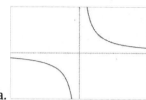
a.

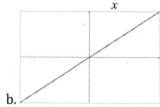
b.

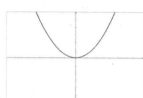
c.

d.

e.

37. What is the determinant of the following matrix?

A = 8x 7y
     3   2x

a. $16x^2 - 21y$
b. $10x + 10y$
c. $16x^2 + 21y$
d. $10x^2 - 10y$
e. $21x + 16y$

38. What is the value of 7! – 3! ?
a. 5,040
b. 5,034
c. 40
d. 4
e. 400

39. Simplify the following expression.
$\sqrt{3}(5\sqrt{3} - \sqrt{12} + \sqrt{10})$
a. $9 + \sqrt{30}$
b. $15 - \sqrt{15} + \sqrt{13}$
c. $15\sqrt{3} - 3\sqrt{12} + 3\sqrt{10}$
d. $3 - \sqrt{13}$
e. $15 - \sqrt{36} + 3\sqrt{30}$

40. Given that $f(x) = 8x + 64$, find the value of $f^1(x)$.
    a. $f^1(x) = -8x - 64$
    b. $f^1(x) = 1/8x - 8$
    c. $f^1(x) = -1/8x -8$
    d. $f^1(x) = x - 8$
    e. $f^1(x) = -x + 8$

41. Based upon the following diagram of a circle, where O is the center and OA and OC are radii:

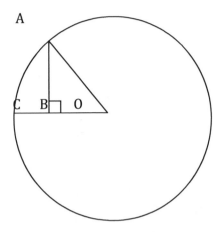

If the length of segment AB = x, and the length of segment OB = y, which of the following expressions describes the radius of the circle?
    a. $x + y$
    b. $x^2 + y^2$
    c. $y + 4$
    d. $\sqrt{x^2 + y^2}$
    e. $\sqrt{x^2 + 1}$

42. What is the surface area, in square inches, of a cube if the length of one side is 3 inches?
    a. 9
    b. 27
    c. 54
    d. 18
    e. 21

43. Which of the following values is closest to the diameter of a circle with an area of 314 square inches?
    a. 20 inches
    b. 10 inches
    c. 100 inches
    d. 31.4 inches
    e. 2π inches

44. For the figure shown, if the length of segment AB is twice the length of segment AD, what is the relationship between segments AC and EC?

a. AC=2EC
b. AC = $\sqrt{2}$ EC
c. EC = $\sqrt{2}$ AC
d. EC = 2AC
e. Cannot be determined.

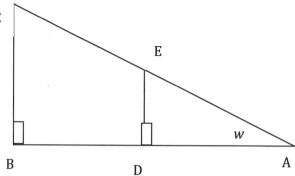

45. A circle is inscribed within a square, as shown. What is the difference between the area of the square and that of the circle, where r is the radius of the circle?

a. 2π
b. $\dfrac{4}{3}\pi r^3$
c. $r^2(4 - \pi)$
d. $2\pi r$
e. $2r^2$

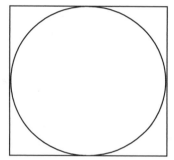

46. Two circles of identical size are adjacent but non-overlapping and are inscribed within a rectangle as shown. If the area of the rectangle is 32 square meters, what is the area of one of the circles?

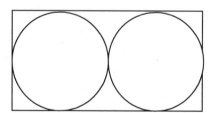

a. 8 m^2
b. 16 m^2
c. 2π m^2
d. 4π m^2
e. Cannot be determined.

47. The town of Fram will build a water storage tank on a hill overlooking the town. The tank will be a right circular cylinder of radius R and height H. The plot of ground selected for the installation is large enough to accommodate a circular tank 60 feet in diameter. The planning commission wants the tank to hold 1,000,000 cubic feet of water, and they intend to use the full area available. Which of the following is the minimum acceptable height?
    a. 655 ft
    b. 455 ft
    c. 355 ft
    d. 255 ft
    e. 155 ft

48. An investigator working for a sporting league suspects that a ball used for one of the contests may have been filled with cork to alter the way it responds when hit. To test his suspicion, he weighs the ball. The density of cork is 3 gm/cm^3, whereas the normal filling has a density of 4 gm/cm^3. The diameter of the ball is 6 cm. If the ball has not been tampered with, how much should it weigh?
    a. 16.75 gm
    b. 113.9 gm
    c. 150.8 gm
    d. 211.45 gm
    e. 24.5 gm

49. Two angles of a triangle measure 15 and 70 degrees, respectively. What is the size of the third angle
    a. 90 degrees
    b. 80 degrees
    c. 75 degrees.
    d. 125 degrees
    e. 95 degrees

50. A circle has a perimeter of 35 feet. What is its diameter?
    a. 11.14 feet
    b. 6.28 feet
    c. 5.57 feet
    d. 3.5 feet
    e. 14 feet.

51. Five numbered equations are plotted on an *x-y* coordinate system in the figure below.

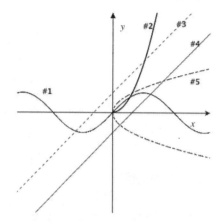

One of these curves corresponds to the equation $y = \sin(x)$. Which one is it?
   a. Curve #1
   b. Curve #2
   c. Curve #3
   d. Curve #4
   e. Curve #5

52. What is the range of the function $y = 3\sin 2x$?
   a. All real numbers
   b. All numbers between -3 and +3
   c. All numbers between -2 and +2
   d. All positive integers
   e. All integers

53. What is the *y* intercept of the function $f(x) = 5 * \cos(3x)$?
   a. (0, 3)
   b. (3, 0)
   c. (5, 3)
   d. (0, 5)
   e. (5, 5)

54. If $f(x) = 3\cos(x) + 5$, what is the value of $f(3°)$?
   a. 2
   b. 6
   c. 8
   d. 14
   e. 4

55. Which of the following paired quantities are equal to one another?
    a. sin (30°) and cos (-30°)
    b. sin $\left(\frac{\pi}{2}\right)$ and 0
    c. cos (45°) and cos (225°)
    d. sin (135°) and $\frac{\sqrt{3}}{2}$
    e. cos (60°) and cos $\left(\frac{-\pi}{3}\right)$

56. What is the length of side BC of the right triangle shown in the figure?

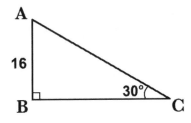

    a. 12
    b. $16\sqrt{2}$
    c. $16\sqrt{3}$
    d. $\frac{16\sqrt{3}}{2}$
    e. 20

57. Comparing the functions $f(\theta) = \cos\theta$ and $g(\theta) = \cos 2\theta$, which of the following statements is true?
    a. The amplitude of one is twice the amplitude of the other.
    b. The period of one is twice the period of the other.
    c. The sum of their squares must equal 1.
    d. $f(\theta) = -\frac{1}{2}g(\theta)$ for $\pi < \theta < \frac{3\pi}{2}$.
    e. $g(\theta) = 2f(\theta)$

58. A line passing through the center of the Earth and the city of Dallas intersects a line drawn through the center of the Earth and the city of Cleveland at an angle of 15°. If the Earth's radius is 6,000 km, what is the distance in km from Dallas to Cleveland?
    a. 1570
    b. 1552
    c. 1525
    d. 1460
    e. 1250

59. The figure below shows a right triangle with one side equal to 12 units. Determine the length of segment C   d. The sine of 15° equals 0.26.

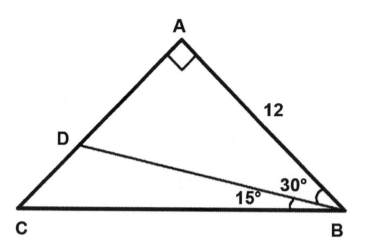

a. 4
b. 6.5
c. 5.08
d. 4.25
e. 6.10

60. Which of the following expressions is symmetric with respect to the y-axis and passes through the point (0,2)?
a. $y = \sin(2x)$
b. $y = \cos(2x)$
c. $y = \tan(2x)$
d. $y = 2\cos(x)$
e. $y = 2\sin(x)$

Answer Key and Explanations

Reading Test

Reading Passage 1

1. **C:** The second paragraph of the passage notes that "up to one-third of people with peanut allergies have severe reactions." Since one-third is approximately 33%, (C) is the correct choice.

2. **E:** The second paragraph of the passage notes that in 2008, Duke experts stated that they expect to offer treatment in five years. Five years from 2008 is 2013.

3. **B:** The last sentence in paragraph five lists the cuisines in which one should watch for peanuts. Italian is not listed.

4. **A:** The second sentence of the first paragraph states that peanut allergy is the most common cause of food-related death.

5. **C:** The passage implies that it is not always easy to know which foods have traces of peanuts in them and that it's important to make sure you know what you're eating. This is hard or impossible if you share someone else's food.

6. **E:** Paragraph two gives examples of symptoms of peanut allergies and, more specifically, examples of symptoms of anaphylaxis. A running or stuffy nose is given as a symptom of the former, but not of the latter.

Reading Passage 2

7. **C:** The first paragraph states that the main purpose of DST it to make better use of daylight.

8. **A:** Energy conservation is discussed as a possible benefit of DST, not a negative effect of it.

9. **D:** The first paragraph states that DST involves setting clocks forward one hour in the spring and one hour backward in the fall.

10. **B:** The last sentence in paragraph four notes that agricultural and evening entertainment interests have historically been opposed to DST.

11. **D:** The passage gives examples of both good and bad effects extra daylight can have on health.

12. **E:** The sixth paragraph notes that DST is observed in only some regions of Brazil.

13. **C:** The last paragraph of the passage notes that DST can lead to peculiar situations, and relays an anecdote about the effect of DST on the birth order of twins.

14. **C:** If $30,000,000 is gained over 7 weeks, each week has a gain of 1/7 of that, or $4,200,000.

15. B: In the second paragraph, the author asserts that Benjamin Franklin suggested DST as a way to save candles.

Reading Passage 3

16. B: You may already know that a conifer is a type of tree. If you do not know this, you can deduce the information based on the fact that the word is used in the description of the Giant Sequoia tree.

17. E: In the first sentence, the passage states that *most* people think the Giant Sequoia is the largest organism. It goes on to explain that there are some people who do not agree.

18. C: The first paragraph describes the General Sherman as the largest Giant Sequoia. The other answer choices include words that can be found in the passage

19. E: If you just glance through, you will see that all of the numbers listed as choices can be found in the passage, but the question asks how many tons the General Sherman is. Only answer choice E, 1400 tons, is correct.

20. E: The passage gives the diameter of the tree at the bottom, but the diameter at the top is not given. You cannot assume the answer, so there is no way to know what the diameter is given the data in the passage.

Reading Passage 4

21. D: Choices A, B, C, and E all have similar meanings and match the text's description of Lubitsch's film style as elegant or sophisticated.

22. C: This phrase is used in the last sentence to describe the Lubitsch style.

23. B: Lubitsch's focus on seemingly irrelevant details as symbols is described in the text as his signature style. (Paragraph 2)

24. C: Lubitsch was invited in 1923 by Albert Zukor.

25. E: Made in 1912, the film could not have been a talkie, as it was not until 1923 that Lubitsch went to Hollywood to use sound technology. And the text tells us nothing of the film's content, personnel, or reception.

26. A: Monescu and Lily were both thieves who posed as members of high society. Mariette was a real heiress, and Lubitsch, of course, was a director, not a character in the film.

27. C: This, indeed, is the underlying theme of the entire movie, as shown by the characters of Monescu and Lily, who appear to be elegant but are, in fact, thieves.

28. B: Lily has no wealth of her own, but Monescu finally chooses her over Mariette and her fortune. (Paragraph 5)

29. B: Lily passes herself off as a countess and Montescu poses as a baron (Paragraph 5).

30. B: Paragraph 6 tells us that he made films in English, German, and French, suggesting that part of his film career was spent in France.

Reading Passage 5

31. C: The passage makes no mention of metals or horses. Although we may infer that they hunted the buffalo because they were plentiful, that is not stated in the passage.

32. B: Travail means work, or effort, and shows that the crows made it more difficult for the people to kill buffalo during the hunt.

33. B: The story tells us that after the great white crow turned black, all the other crows were black as well. Thus, he is a symbol for all these birds.

34. D: The third paragraph tells us that the tribe planned to frighten the chief of the crows to prevent the crows from warning the buffalo about the hunts. The passage does not suggest that they hated all birds or that they planned to eat this one.

35. C: Long Arrow acted like the buffalo in the herd so that the chief of the crows would approach, making it possible to capture him. Although we may infer that he had to fool the buffalo in the herd as well, this is secondary to his need to fool the birds.

36. B: These details help us to see how the people lived. Although they hunted with the stone-tipped spears, the rawhide bag was not a part of the hunt.

37. A: As he lands, he asks "have you not heard my warning?" (Paragraph 7).

38. A: The suggestions included several for killing or mutilating the bird, which does not suggest a calm resolve or jubilation. And there is no suggestion that they were either celebrating or hungry at this time.

39. D: There is no characterization of Long Arrow in the passage, and we know nothing about him or why he was chosen.

40. B: The birds in the story are able to observe the actions of hunters, to interpret them as potentially harmful for their buffalo friends, and to act for the protection of the buffalo. They do not appear to do this for their own benefit, nor do they seem to act specifically to harm the tribe, but rather to help the buffalo.

Reading Passage 6

41. B: The first paragraph refers to the Spray as a sloop, which is a kind of sailboat, and refers to its being berthed among the docks.

42. B: In the first paragraph the author describes his surprise at the changes in the harbor, and indicates that the changes downtown were much less.

43. C: Paragraph 2 opens by mentioning a letter of introduction that had been sent ahead from another of the author's contacts in Montevideo.

44. C: Paragraph 2 mentions the "Standard's" columns, which had contained stories about the Spray's voyage.

- 127 -

45. B: Although "landmarks" are usually monuments or buildings, the author uses the term and goes on to describe a number of merchants who had been present during his earlier visit to the city, and who were significant features of the town in his estimation.

46. C: Paragraph 3 tells us that the lemons "went on forever," suggesting that the merchant hardly ever changed them at all.

47. B: The author would have liked to look up the whiskey merchant, but there is nothing in the passage to suggest that he was desperate or anxious to do so.

48. C: The phrase in paragraph 4, that the waters were "not entirely blameless of the germs of disease," indicates that some germs may have been present in them.

49. B: Throughout the passage, the author is looking for people he had seen on his first visit, and he says of this merchant that he had "survived" (Paragraph 5).

50. A: Since the sign has been present since the author's previous visit to the city, we may infer that the merchant is not really concerned about an imminent comet strike. And the wording of the sign suggests that his wares are for sale "at any price."

Reading Passage 7
51. B: Cilia and flagella are both organelles, which are defined in the first paragraph as sub-cellular structures that perform a particular function.

52. A: The second paragraph describes the function of cilia as providing fluid flow across the gills or the epithelia lining the digestive tract. The stomach is part of the digestive tract.

53. C: The third paragraph of the text describes 9 peripheral pairs of polymers, and two central ones, or 20 in all.

54. B: Tubulin and dynein are both defined as proteins in the text (Paragraphs 3 and 4). Flagellin is a protein, but it is not mentioned in the text. Sonneborn is not a protein; he was a scientist.

55. B: The mechanism is explained in detail in the fourth paragraph. Dynein causes the outer polymer pairs to slide past each other, not to bend. The inner polymers do not have dynein associated with them, so they are not involved in the bending. And the passage cites no evidence to suggest that the organelles contract. While "flagella beat in a circular, undulating motion that is continuous" (Paragraph 2), the question is asking for an explanation of this movement, not a description.

56. C: Although the polymers in this passage are made of protein subunits, the definition is more general. Paragraph 3 tells us that in this case the subunits are tubulin proteins.

57. B: The fourth paragraph introduces Sonneborn as "of Indiana University" and describes him doing scientific research.

58. D: The experiment described in Paragraph 5 showed that the cilia always retained their original direction of rotation.

59. D: The first paragraph states that both structures are less than 5 μm in diameter.

60. B: Sonneborn performed his experiment with cilia, not with flagella.

Writing Test

Passage 1

1. C: In the original text, the word "would" is slang and adds nothing to the sentence. Answers B, D, and E differ in meaning from the original.

2. D: The hyphens clarify the meaning by showing that the entire three-word clause modifies the expression "food supply."

3. B: By separating the modifying clause "in recent years," it clarifies the meaning of the sentence.

4. B: The original does not specify who is referred to by the word "their," which is unnecessary. Answer D is incorrect usage.

5. B: The word "that" has already appeared ("It seems logical that...") and is redundant if used again here.

6. A: None of the other spellings make sense in this usage.

7. A: The percentage plainly refers to the population mentioned earlier in the sentence. All the other answers are redundant.

8. B: Answer B is the possessive of a plural noun. The original text offers the possessive of a singular noun, which is incorrect. The other answers are not possessives. Also, "United States" is a proper noun and remains capitalized.

9. B: Answer B is the simplest. The word "still" in the original suggests that people will not buy expensive foods even if some other condition is met, but no such condition is specified. Therefore, the word is unnecessary and confusing.

10. B: The word "your" in the original is slang usage. Answer C is incorrect because it is a plural, not a possessive.

11. D: In this case, "too" means "also."

12. B: The phrase is redundant since the word "theory" is included in the name "the paycheck cycle theory" which follows immediately afterwards in the sentence.

13. C: The word "family" is used redundantly in the original sentence, and is easily replaced by a pronoun in this case.

14. C: The hypothesis suggests the *existence* of a cycle that promotes weight gain. In the original, the word "that" makes the sentence nonsensical.

15. C: The use of "would" in the original is slang. The author is saying that, if the paycheck cycle hypothesis is correct, the two causes of overweight are periodic food restriction and poor diet. Since there is some uncertainty here, C is a better choice than B.

Passage 2

1. C: Answer C is the possessive of the plural noun "women."

2. C: Answer C is a possessive. Answer D and answer E are technically correct, but it is common usage to use these expressions as collective nouns, so that "porter's lodge" can describe a lodge for more than one porter.

3. C: The other answers do not make sense.

4. A: The original maintains the singular present tense required for this sentence. Choice B indicates past tense, while the preceding and following paragraphs indicate present tense. While option C is present tense, the subject is singular and requires a singular verb. Answers D (Present perfect tense) and E (Future tense) are incorrect.

5. B: Answer C changes the meaning, suggesting that the action is not performed every day, whereas the original text indicates that it occurs daily but that the time is indefinite.

6. A: "Entryway" is the correct spelling.

7. B: The phrase in the original is unnecessary, and is redundant as it repeats "only." The other answers are unnecessarily wordy.

8. C: The original text splits the infinitive "to receive." Answers B and D imply that this happens all the time, whereas the text implies that it is an exceptional occurrence. Answer E is an incorrect spelling of "receive."

9. D: Answer C repeats the word "even" and is redundant.

10. B: The original text and answer E is phrased awkwardly, and answers C and D change the meaning.

11. B: This provides a parallel construction between "morning" and "evening."

12. C: The original seeks to imply that the guards are not effectively on watch, but the phrasing is awkward and makes no sense. Answer B is correctly spelled, but retains the awkward phrasing of the original.

13. D: Since all the elements of the list contain verbs, this choice provides for parallel construction by also including the verb. Answer C and answer E are less desirable, since the combination of "physically" and "out of shape" is redundant.

14. B: The other choices are unnecessarily wordy.

15. D: Answer D most specifically explains what has been ineffective about the tactics of the guards. Answer C and answer E are vague.

Passage 3

1. A: Capitalization is required since the school name is a proper noun, and a possessive is needed since the program belongs to the school.

2. B: The infinitive ("to do") should always be used in the present tense.

3. C: The infinitive ("to afford") should always be used in the present tense.

4. B: The original is redundant, since "at last" and "finally" have the same meaning.

5. C: The original version is awkward, since it repeats the word "soon" which appeared earlier in the same sentence.

6. A: The comma is not required before a subordinating conjunction such as "until."

7. D: The commas are used to set off Dr. Ed Cook's name as a parenthetical element.

8. C: In the original version, the word "this" is slang usage.

9. C: The original version is nonsensical, and none of the other answers are grammatically correct.

10. B: Answer C is grammatically correct, but the phrase adds nothing to the author's description of the purpose of the work done on board the boat.

11. C: The original version (needlessly wordy), answer B, and answer E contain the assumption that the tests will be successful. Answers C and D are more precise in that they do not make this assumption, but D repeats the word "test," so that C is the better choice.

12. B: In the original version, "these" is slang usage. Answers C, D, and E are grammatically correct but needlessly vague.

13. C: This sentence is completely unrelated to the material that precedes it in the paragraph, which warrants beginning a new one.

14. D: This is an example of slang usage and is exceedingly vague. If the author wanted to indicate that the fish were interested in the ship's lights and in other things, as well, one or more examples should have been given.

15. C: Answer C provides the same information as the other choices but is far more concise.

Passage 4

1. C: Answer C is correct as this phrase tells the reader where the man appeared. Answer A creates a run-on sentence, answers B and E are redundant, and choice D creates a disagreement of verb tense.

2. B: The original and answer C are slang usage. Answers D and E are incorrect; they suggest that the villagers had only then noticed the monkeys.

3. B: As the clause following the conjunction *and* is dependent, the comma is not employed.

4. D: The action described in the portion of the sentence following the conjunction is contrary to expectation, since the villagers hunted less despite the generous payments, and *but* reflects that contradiction better than any of the other choices.

5. D: The correct spelling for the possessive pronoun.

6. C: Answer C implies that the action that follows is a consequence of the one that precedes, i.e., the man raised his price because the villagers were losing interest.

7. A: No comma is used to set off this dependent clause.

8. C: Answer C is an adjective indicating finite supply. Answer A is an adverb, inappropriate for modifying a noun.

9. B: Answer B avoids splitting the infinitive "to see" while maintaining the emphasis provided by "even."

10. C: This proper use of the infinitive also maintains parallel structure with "to see," which appears earlier in the same sentence.

11. B: A semi-colon may be used to join two sentences when they are of similar content.

12. D: Using the subjective pronoun *he* with the verb *to be*. Answers B, C, and E create a repetitive structure within the paragraph.

13. B: Answer B uses the subjective pronoun *I* with the verb *to be*.

14. C: The past tense is needed since the story is set in the past. Answer D is slang usage.

15. A: The comma appropriately sets off the ending clause and adds emphasis. Answer B is a run-on sentence, while C, D, and E introduce changes in meaning.

Math Test

1. C: 16.5 x 4/3 = 22.

2. D: An easy way to do this is to remember that for a number to be divisible by 3, the sum of the digits must be divisible by 3. Thus, for 555, 5+5+5=15, and 15/3 = 5. 555/3 = 185

3. D: Distance is the product of velocity and time, and (5×10^6) x 2×10^{-4} = $(10 \times 10^6 \times 10^{-4})$ = 10^3=1000.

4. B: 25% off is equivalent to $25 \times \dfrac{\$138}{100} = \$34.50$, so the sale price becomes $138 - $34.50 = $103.50.

5. C: The expression 2^{-3} is equivalent to $\dfrac{1}{2^3}$, and since $2^3 = 8$, it is equivalent to 1/8.

6. B: 30% 0f 3300 = 0.3 x 3300 = 990

7. B: The value of the fraction $\dfrac{7}{5}$ can be evaluated by dividing 7 by 5, which yields 1.4. The average of 1.4 and 1.4 is $\dfrac{1.4 + 1.4}{2} = 1.4$.

8. E: $(3x^{-2})^3 = 3^3 \times (x^{-2})^3 = 27 \times (\dfrac{1}{x^2})^3 = 27 \times \dfrac{1}{x^6} = 27 x^{-6}$

9. B: The lowest score, 68, is eliminated. The average of the remaining four grades is

$$Avg = \dfrac{75 + 88 + 86 + 90}{4} = 84.75$$

Rounding up to the nearest integer gives a final grade of 85. Since this value is unique, all the other answers are incorrect.

10. A: The band's share, 25% of $20,000,000, is $5,000,000. After the agent's share is subtracted, the band gets $(1 - 0.15) \times \$5,000,000 = 0.85 \times \$5,000,000 = \$4,250,000$ and each band member gets one fifth of that, or $850,000. Since this value is unique, all the other answers are incorrect.

11. B: Distance traveled is the product of velocity and time, or
$D = 3 \times 10^{-11} \times 1 \times 10^6 = (3 \times 1) \times (10^{-11} \times 10^6) = 3 \times 10^{-5}$ meters. Since this value is unique, all the other answers are incorrect.

12. B: The median is the value in a group of numbers that separates the upper half from the lower half, so that there are an equal number of values above and below it. In this distribution, there are two values greater than 116, and two values below it.

13. D: The product $(a)(a)(a)(a)(a)$ is defined as a to the fifth power.

14. B: $7.5 \times 10^{-4} = \dfrac{7.5}{10,000} = 0.00075$

Since this value is unique, all the other answers are incorrect.

15. B: A prime number is a natural, positive, non-zero number which can be factored only by itself and by 1. This is the case for 11.

16. C

17. E: The fraction of those playing drums plus the fraction of those playing a brass instrument must total 1. So the number that play drums is pn, and the number playing brass must be $(1-p)n$.

18. A: Explanation: Since the second line, $y = 3$, is a vertical, the intersection must occur at a point where $y = 3$. If x = -1.5, the equation describing the line is satisfied: $(2 \times [-1.5] + 3) = 0$

19. A: For the line to be parallel to the x-axis, the slope must be 0. This condition is met if y has a constant value.

20. A: As defined, the line will be described by the equation $y = 4x + 1$. Expression A fits this equation ($9 = 4 \times 2 + 1$). The others do not.

21. A: The vertical operators indicate absolute values, which are always positive. Thus, $|\,7\text{-}5\,| = 2$, and $|\,5\text{-}7\,| = |\,\text{-}2\,| = 2$, and $2 - 2 = 0$.

22. E: Each term of each expression in parentheses must be multiplied by each term in the other.
　　　Thus for E, $(x + 3)(3x - 5) = 3x^2 + 9x - 5x - 15 = 3x^2 + 4x - 15$

23. A: From the starting expression, compute:
$3(\dfrac{6x - 3}{3}) - 3(9x + 9) = 3(2x - 1) - 27x - 27 = 6x - 3 - 27x - 27 = -21x - 30 = -3(7x + 10)$

24. B: Compute as follows: $(3 - 2 \times 2)^2 = (3 - 4)^2 = (-1)^2 = 1$.

25. A: Each glass of lemonade costs 10¢, or \$0.10, so that g glasses will cost $g \times \$0.10$. To this, add Bob's fixed cost of \$45, giving the expression in A.

26. B: To calculate S, calculate the discount and subtract it from the original price, p. The discount is 33% of p, or $0.33p$. Thus, $S = p - 0.33p$.

27. A: Rearranging the equation gives $x^2 = -1$. However, the square of a real number cannot yield a negative result, so no real number solutions exist for the equation.

28. C: Rearranging the equation gives
$3(x+4) = 15(x-5)$, which is equivalent to
$15x - 3x = 12 + 75$, or
$12x = 87$, and solving for x,
$$x = \frac{87}{12} = \frac{29}{4}.$$

29. D: Let P_A = the price of truck A and P_B that of truck b. Similarly let M_A and M_B represent the gas mileage obtained by each truck. The total cost of driving a truck n miles is
$$C = P + n \times \frac{\$4}{M}$$
To determine the break-even mileage, set the two cost equations equal to one another and solve for n:
$$P_A + n \times \frac{\$4}{M_A} = P_B + n \times \frac{\$4}{M_B}$$
$$n \times (\frac{\$4}{M_A} - \frac{\$4}{M_B}) = P_B - P_A$$
$$n = \frac{P_B - P_A}{(\frac{\$4}{M_A} - \frac{\$4}{M_B})}$$
Plugging in the given values:
$$n = \frac{650 - 450}{(\frac{4}{25} - \frac{4}{35})} = \frac{200}{(0.16 - 0.11)} = 740 \text{ miles.}$$

30. B: First determine the proportion of students in Grade 5. Since the total number of students is 180, this proportion is $\frac{36}{180} = 0.2$, or 20%. Then determine the same proportion of the total prizes, which is 20% of twenty, or $0.2 \times 20 = 4$.

31. B: The easiest pair to test is the third: $y = 4$ and $x = 0$. Substitute these values in each of the given equations and evaluate. Choice B gives $4 = 0 + 4$, which is a true statement. None of the other answer choices is correct this number set.

32. A: Evaluate as follows: $2f(x) - 3 = 2(2x^2 + 7) - 3 = 4x^2 + 14 - 3 = 4x^2 + 11$

33. C: Explanation: This can be solved as two equations with two unknowns. Since the integers are consecutive with $p > n$, we have $p - n = 1$, so that $p = 1 + n$. Substituting this value into $p + n = 15$ gives $1 + 2n = 15$, or $n = \frac{14}{2} = 7$.

34. D: At the point of intersection, the y-coordinates are equal on both lines so that $2x + 3 = x - 5$. Solving for x, we have $x = -8$. Then, evaluating y with either equation yields
$y = 2(-8) + 3 = -16 + 3 = -13$ or $y = -8 - 5 = -13$

35. B: Simply evaluating the expression yields

$$y(15) = -\frac{1}{2}(32)(15)^2 + 0 + 30{,}000 = -\frac{1}{2}(32)(225) + 0 + 30{,}000 = -3{,}600 + 30{,}000$$
$$= 26{,}400\text{ft}$$

36. A: This is a typical plot of an inverse variation, in which the product of the dependent and independent variables, x and y, is always equal to the same value. In this case the product is always equal to 1, so the plot occupies the first and third quadrants of the coordinate plane. As x increases and approaches infinity, , y decreases and approaches zero, maintaining the constant product.

37. A: $A = \begin{matrix} 8x & 7y \\ 3 & 2x \end{matrix}$

To find the determinant, multiply the top left corner by the bottom right corner. Then subtract the product of the bottom left corner and the top right corner.
$(8x \cdot 2x) - (7y \cdot 3)$
$16x^2 - 21y$

38. B: $7! - 3! =$
To evaluate:
$(1 \times 2 \times 3 \times 4 \times 5 \times 6 \times 7) - (1 \times 2 \times 3) =$
$5{,}040 - 6 = 5{,}034$

39. A: $\sqrt{3}(5\sqrt{3} - \sqrt{12} + \sqrt{10})$
To simplify, all terms inside the brackets must be multiplied by $\sqrt{3}$
$5\sqrt{3} \times \sqrt{3} - \sqrt{3} \times \sqrt{12} + \sqrt{10} \times \sqrt{3}$
According to the order of operations, multiplication is completed first.
$5\sqrt{9} - \sqrt{36} + \sqrt{30}$
Since the square root of 9 and 36 are whole numbers, this expression can be further simplified.
$5 \times 3 - 6 + \sqrt{30}$
$15 - 6 + \sqrt{30}$
$9 + \sqrt{30}$

40. B: There are several ways to find the inverse of a function. One way is to switch the y and x in the equation and then solve for x.
$f(x) = 8x + 64$
$y = 8x + 64$
Switch the x and y
$x = 8y + 64$
Then, solve for y.
$-8y = -x + 64$
$y = 1/8x - 8$
This is the value of $f^{-1}(x)$.

41. D: The radius r of this circle is the line O   a. Since B is a right angle, OA is the hypotenuse and by the Pythagorean theorem, $r^2 = x^2 + y^2$ so that $r = \sqrt{x^2 + y^2}$.

42. C: The surface of a cube is obtained by multiplying the area of each face by 6, since there are 6 faces. The area of each face is the square of the length of one edge. Therefore
$A = 6 \times 3^2 = 6 \times 9 = 54$.

43. A: The area A of a circle is given by $A = \pi \times r^2$, where r is the radius. Since π is approximately 3.14, we can solve for $r = \sqrt{\dfrac{A}{\pi}} = \sqrt{\dfrac{314}{3.14}} = \sqrt{100} = 10$. Now, the diameter d is twice the radius, or $d = 2 \times 10 = 20$.

44. A: This is evident if the line EG is drawn parallel to segment BD,

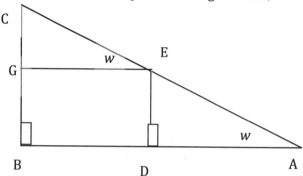

First, note that if AB is twice the length of AD then, since AB = AD + DB, it follows that AB is also twice the length of DB (AB = 2 DB). It can be seen that angle w at the vertice E is the same as the angle w at vertice A, so that the cosines of these two angles must be the same. This gives $\dfrac{AB}{AC} = \dfrac{EG}{EC}$, and since DB = EG, it follows that $\dfrac{AB}{AC} = \dfrac{DB}{EC}$, which is equivalent to $\dfrac{AC}{AB} = \dfrac{EC}{DB}$. Now, since AB = 2 DB, $\dfrac{AC}{2 \times DB} = \dfrac{EC}{DB}$. Rearranging $EC = \dfrac{DB \times AC}{2 \times DB}$, and simplifying gives $EC = \dfrac{AC}{2}$, or AC = 2 EC.

45. C: The side of the square is equal to the diameter of the circle, or twice the radius, that is, $2r$. The area of the square is this quantity squared, or $4r^2$. The area of the circle is, πr^2. Subtracting gives the difference between the two areas,
$$\Delta A = 4r^2 - \pi r^2 = r^2(4 - \pi).$$

46. D: The vertical sides of the rectangle are equal to $2r$, where r is the radius of the circles (see Figure). Similarly, the horizontal side of the rectangle is equal to $4r$. Thus, the area of the rectangle is $A_R = 2r \times 4r = 8r^2$. If this equals 32 square meters, as given, then solve for r:

$$8r^2 = 32$$
$$r^2 = \frac{32}{8} = 4$$

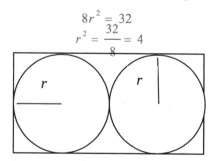

so that $r = \sqrt{4} = 2$. Therefore, the area of a circle $A_c = \pi r^2 = 4\pi$.

47. C: The volume of a right circular cylinder is equal to its height multiplied by the area of its base, a. Since the base is circular, $A = \pi R^2$, where R, the radius, is half the diameter, or 30 feet. Therefore,

$$V = H \times \pi R^2$$

Solving for H,

$$H = \frac{V}{\pi R^2} = \frac{1,000,000}{\pi \times 30^2} = \frac{1,000,000}{\pi \times 900} = 353.7 \text{ ft}$$

48. C: The weight of the ball, W, is the product of the density, d, and the volume, V. Since a ball is a sphere, and the radius is half the diameter, the volume is $V = \frac{4}{3}\pi r^3$, so that

$$W = d \times \frac{4}{3}\pi r^3 = 4 \times \frac{4}{3}\pi \times 9 = 150.8 \text{ gm.}$$

49. E: The sum of angles in a triangle equals 180 degrees. Therefore solve for the remaining angle as 180 – (15 + 70) = 95 degrees.

50. A: The perimeter of a circle is given by $2\pi r$, where r is the radius. We solve for $r = \frac{35}{2\pi} = 5.57$, and double this value to obtain the diameter $d = 11.14$ feet.

51. A: The sine function is a periodic function whose value oscillates between 1 and -1 just as Curve #1 does.

52. B: The range of a function is all of the possible values for x. In a standard sine curve, the range is -1 to +1. In the function $y = 3\sin 2x$, there is a vertical stretch of 3. Therefore, the range of this function is all values between -3 and +3.

53. D: $f(x) = 5 \cos(3x)$
A cosine curve usually intercepts the y-axis at (0,1). However, this cosine curve has a vertical stretch of 5, meaning the y-value of the point of interception must be multiplied by 5. Therefore (0, 1 × 5)
The y-intercept is (0,5)

54. C: $f(x) = 3\cos(x) + 5$
To find $f(3°)$, it is simply a matter of substituting 3° for x.
$f(3) = 3\cos(3°) + 5$
$f(3) = 3 \times 0.9986 + 5$
$f(3) = 8$

55. E: Negative angles in the fourth quadrant have the same cosine values as the corresponding positive angles in the first quadrant. Since $\frac{\pi}{3}$ radians equals 60°, we have cos (60°) = cos (-60°) = 0.5.

56. C: This can be solved either by determining the cotangent of 30° or by applying the law of sines. In the first case, $\cot(30°) = \frac{BC}{16}$, so that BC = 16 cot(30°). Since $\cot(30°) = \frac{\cos(30°)}{\sin(30°)} = \sqrt{3}$, the

solution is $16\sqrt{3}$. To use the law of sines, note that angle A must equal 60° since the sum of angles in a triangle is 180°. Now, from the law of sines, $\frac{16}{\sin(30°)} = \frac{BC}{\sin(60°)}$, from which it may be determined that $BC = \frac{16\sin(30°)}{\sin(30°)} = 16\sqrt{3}$.

57. B: Trigonometric functions are said to be *periodic,* that is, they oscillate regularly between a maximum and minimum value. The difference between the maximum or minimum and the baseline is termed the *amplitude* of the function. For a cosine, the maximum is 1 and the minimum is -1, so that the amplitude is equal to 1. The *period* is simply the length of a full cycle. This is shown in the following diagram, where $f(\theta) = \cos\theta$ is plotted as a solid line, and $g(\theta) = \cos 2\theta$ is plotted as a broken line.

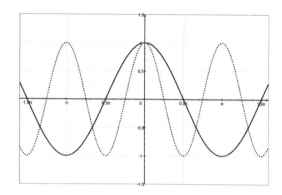

58. A: The circumference of the Earth along any great circle is equal to $2\pi r$, where r is the radius. This yields 37,700 km for a radius of 6,000 km. Since the angle subtending the arc that separates the two cities is 15°, the following proportion holds if the arc length is represented by d:
$\frac{d}{37,700} = \frac{15}{360}$. Solving for d yields $d = \frac{15 \cdot 37,700}{360} = 1570\ km$.

59. C: This problem can be solved either with the law of sines or by determining the tangent of 30°. First, since the sum of the two angles at vertex B is 45°, it follows that the angle C is also 45° (since the sum of internal angles of a triangle equals 180°). Therefore triangle ABC is isosceles and side AC equals side AB and is 12 units long. Therefore, CD = 12 – A   d. The length of AD can be determined from the tangent of 30°, since $\frac{AD}{AB} = \tan(30°) = \frac{1}{\sqrt{3}}$. Now, since AB = 12, $AD = \frac{12}{\sqrt{3}} = 6.92$, and therefore CD = 12 – 6.92 = 5.08.

An alternative solution comes from the law of sines. As shown above, AC = 12, so that from the Pythagorean relationship it can be determined that $CB = \sqrt{12^2 + 12^2} = \sqrt{288} = 12\sqrt{2}$. Since the angle at C is 45°, it follows that angle CDB = 120°. Applying the law of sines, $\frac{CD}{\sin(15°)} = \frac{CB}{\sin(120°)}$. This yields $CD = \frac{12\sqrt{2}\cdot\sin(15°)}{\sin(60°)} = 5.08$.

60. D: Of the functions shown, only the cosine is symmetric with respect to the *y*-axis, since none of the others have a maximum or a minimum at $x = 0$. To pass through the point (0,2), the function must have a value of $y = 2$ where $x = 0$. Since cos (0) = 1, it follows that 2 cos(0) = 2.